THE LOTUS SUTRA OF THE TRUE DHARMA

D1737997

Contents

INTRODUCTION   iv
THE LOTUS SUTRA OF TRUE DHARMA   1
   PART I.   1
   PART II.   22
   PART III.   45
   PART IV.   73
   PART V.   87
   PART VI.   103
   PART VII.   111
   PART VIII.   138
   PART IX.   148
   PART X.   154
   PART XI.   163
   PART XII.   182
   PART XIII.   187

INTRODUCTION

The Lotus Sutra of the True Dharma, more commonly known in English as the Lotus Sutra (Sanskrit: *Saddharma-Puṇḍarīka-Sūtra*), is one of the most revered and significant Mahayana Buddhist texts of East Asia. It contains the teachings of Gautama Buddha, enlightened teacher and sage who lived and taught in the northeastern part of ancient India in approximately 5th century BCE. It is believed that Buddha gave this teaching during the last period of his life, proclaiming the ultimate principles of the Dharma and uniting all previous teachings into one. With many parables the Buddha teaches that all beings can become fully enlightened and that this achievement, and not that of becoming Shravakas or Pratyekabuddhas, has always been the ultimate intent of his teaching.

The narrative in the Lotus Sutra captures the second turning of the wheel of Dharma, an event of great importance in Buddhism for all sentient beings. This sutra also became the tenet on which the Tiantai, Tendai, Cheontae, and Nichiren schools of Buddhism were established and is known for its extensive instruction on the concept and usage of skillful means – the seventh Paramita or perfection of a Bodhisattva. According to British professor Paul Williams: "For many East Asian Buddhists since early times, the Lotus Sutra contains the final teaching of the Buddha, complete and sufficient for salvation."

This particular English translation of the Lotus Sutra is from Johan H.Kern's *Sacred Books of the East, Vol XXI* published in 1884. As one of the earliest English translations of any of the Buddhist Sutras, the text was adapted to be more comprehensible for the society at the time. Some adjustments were made to the original translation to make the terminology more consistent and to include elements found in the Sanskrit text.

May the Lotus Sutra bring you a gift of peace, joy and unshakable inner freedom.

THE LOTUS SUTRA OF TRUE DHARMA

PART I.

INTRODUCTORY.

THUS HAVE I HEARD. Once upon a time Bhagavat was staying at Ragagriha, on the Gridhrakuta mountain, with a numerous assemblage of monks, twelve hundred monks, all of them Arhats (advanced enlightened beings), free from depravity, self-controlled, thoroughly emancipated in thought and knowledge, of noble breed, like-unto great elephants, having done their task, done their duty, acquitted their charge, reached the goal; in whom the ties which bound them to existence were wholly destroyed, whose minds were thoroughly emancipated by perfect knowledge, who had reached the utmost perfection in subduing all their thoughts; who were possessed of the transcendent faculties; eminent disciples, such as the venerable Agnata-Kaundinya, the venerable Asvagit, the venerable Vashpa, the venerable Mahanaman, the venerable Bhadrikal, the venerable Maha-Kasyapa, the venerable Kasyapa of Uruvilva, the venerable Kasyapa of Nadi,

1

the venerable Kasyapa of Gaya, the venerable Sariputra, the venerable Maha-Maudgalyayana, the venerable Maha-Katyayana, the venerable Aniruddha, the venerable Revata, the venerable Kapphina, the venerable Gavampati, the venerable Pilindavatsa, the venerable Vakula, the venerable Bharadvaga, the venerable Maha-Kaushthila, the venerable Nanda, the venerable Upananda, the venerable Sundara-Nanda, the venerable Purna Maitrayaniputra, the venerable Subhuti, the venerable Rahula; with them yet other great disciples, as the venerable Ananda, still under training, and two thousand other monks, some of whom still under training, the others masters; with six thousand nuns having at their head Mahapragapati, and the nun Yasodhara, the mother of Rahula, along with her train; further with eighty thousand Bodhisattvas, all unable to slide back, endowed with the spells of supreme, perfect enlightenment, firmly standing in wisdom; who moved onward the never deviating wheel of the Dharma law; who had propitiated many hundred thousands of Buddhas; who under many hundred thousands of Buddhas had planted the roots of goodness, had been intimate with many hundred thousands of Buddhas, were in body and mind fully penetrated with the feeling of charity; able in communicating the wisdom of the Tathagatas (perfected beings; 'One who has gone'); very wise, having reached the perfection of wisdom; renowned in many hundred thousands of worlds; having saved many hundred thousand myriads of kotis of beings; such as the Bodhisattva Mahasattva Mangusri, as prince royal; the Bodhisattvas Mahasattvas Avalokitesvara, Mahasthamaprapta, Sarvarthanaman, Nityodyukta, Anikshiptadhura, Ratnakandra, Bhaishagyaraga, Pradanasura, Ratnakandra, Ratnaprabha, Purnakandra, Mahivikramin, Trailokavikramin, Anantavikramin, Mahapratibhana, Satatasamitabhiyukta, Dharanidhara, Akshayamati, Padmasri, Nakshatraraga, the Bodhisattva Mahasattva Maitreya, the Bodhisattva Mahasattva Simha.

With them were also the sixteen virtuous men to begin with Bhadrapala, to wit, Bhadrapala, Ratnikara, Susarthavaha, Naradatta, Guhagupta, Varunadatta, Indradatta, Uttaramati, Viseshamati, Vardhamanamati, Amoghadarsin, Susamsthita, Suvikrantavikramin, Anupamamati, Suryagarbha, and Dharanidhara; besides eighty thousand Bodhisattvas, among whom the fore-mentioned were the chiefs; further Sakra, the ruler of the celestials, with twenty thousand gods, his followers, such as the god Kandra (the Moon, alternative spelling: Chandra), the god Surya (the Sun), the god Samantagandha (the Wind), the god Ratnaprabha, the god Avabhasaprabha, and others; further, the four great rulers of the cardinal points with thirty thousand gods in their train: the great ruler Virudhaka, the great ruler Virupaksha, the great ruler Dhritarashtra, and the great ruler Vaisravana; the god Isvara and the god Mahesvara, each followed by thirty thousand gods; further, Brahma Sahdmpati and his twelve thousand followers, the BrahmakAyika gods, amongst whom Brahma Sikhin and Brahma Gyotishprabha, with the other twelve thousand Brahmakdyika gods; together with the eight Naga kings and many hundred thousand myriads of kotis of Nigas in their train, viz. the Naga king Nanda, the Naga king Upananda, Sagara, Vasuki, Takshaka, Manasvin, Anavatapta, and Utpalaka; further, the four Kinnara kings with many hundred thousand myriads of kotis of followers, viz. the Kinnara king Druma, the Kinnara king Mahadharma, the Kinnara king Sudharma, and the Kinnara king Dharmadhara; besides, the four divine beings called Gandharvakayikas with many hundred thousand Gandharvas in their suite, viz. the Gandharva Manogna, the Gandharva Manognasvara, the Gandharva Madhura, and the Gandharva Madhurasvara; further, the four chiefs of the demons followed by many hundred thousand myriads of kotis of demons, viz. the chief of the demons Bali, Kharaskandha, Vemakitri, and Rahu; along with the four Garuda chiefs followed by many hundred thousand myriads of kotis of Garudas, viz. the Garuda chiefs Mahategas, Mahakaya, Mahapurna, and Maharddhiprapta, and with Agatasatru, king of Magadha, the son of Vaidehi.

Now at that time the Bhagavat was surrounded, attended, honoured, revered, venerated, worshipped by the four classes of hearers, after expounding the Dharmaparyaya called the Great Exposition, a text of great development, serving to instruct Bodhisattvas and proper to all Buddhas, sat cross-legged on the seat of the law and entered upon the meditation termed 'the station of the exposition of Infinity'. His body was motionless and his mind had reached perfect tranquillity. And as soon as Bhagavat had entered upon his meditation, there fell a great rain of divine flowers, Mandaravasa and great Mandaravas, Mangushakas and great Mangushakas, covering Bhagavat and the four classes of hearers, while the whole Buddha field shook in six ways: it moved, removed, trembled, trembled from one end to the other, tossed, tossed along.

Then did those who were assembled and sitting together in that congregation, monks, nuns, male and female lay devotees, gods, Nagas, goblins, Gandharvas, demons, Garudas, Kinnaras, great serpents, men, and beings not human, as well as governors of a region, rulers of armies and rulers of four continents, all of them with their followers, gaze on Bhagavat in astonishment, in amazement, in ecstasy.

And at that moment there issued a ray from within the circle of hair between the eyebrows of Bhagavat. It extended over eighteen hundred thousand Buddha-fields in the eastern quarter, so that all those Buddha-fields appeared wholly illuminated by its radiance, down to the great hell Aviki and up to the limit of existence. And the beings in any of the six states of existence became visible, all without exception. Likewise the Buddhas staying, living, and existing in those Buddha-fields became all visible, and the Dhamrma preached by them could be entirely heard by all beings. And the monks, nuns, lay devotees male and female, Yogins and students of Yoga, those who had obtained the fruition of the Paths of sanctification and those who had not, they, too, became visible. And the Bodhisattvas Mahasattvas in those Buddha-fields who plied the Bodhisattva-course with ability, due to their earnest belief in numerous and various lessons and the fundamental ideas, they, too, became all visible. Likewise the Buddhas in those Buddha-fields who had reached final Nirvana became visible, all of them. And the Stupas made of jewels and containing the relics of the extinct Buddhas became all visible in those Buddha-fields.

Then rose in the mind of the Bodhisattva Mahasattva Maitreya this thought: 'O how great a wonder does the Tathagata display! What may be the cause, what the reason of Bhagavat producing so great a wonder as this? And such astonishing, prodigious, inconceivable, powerful miracles now appear, although Bhagavat is absorbed in meditation! Why, let me inquire about this matter; who would be able here to explain it to me?'

He then thought: 'Here is Mangusri, the royal prince, who has plied his office under former Jinas (Arhats, advanced enlightened beings) and planted the roots of goodness, while worshipping many Buddhas. This Mangusri must have witnessed before such signs of the former Tathagatas, those Arhats, those perfectly enlightened Buddhas; for a long time he must have enjoyed the grand conversations on the Dharma law. Therefore will I inquire about this matter with Mangusri.'

And the four classes of the audience, monks, nuns, male and female lay devotees, numerous gods, Nagas, goblins, Gandharvas, demons, Garudas, Kinnaras, great serpents, men, and beings not human, on seeing the magnificence of this great miracle of the Bhagavat, were struck with astonishment, amazement and curiosity, and thought: 'Let us inquire why this magnificent miracle has been produced by the great power of Bhagavat.'

At the same moment, at that very instant, the Bodhisattva Mahasattva Maitreya knew in his mind the thoughts arising in the minds of the four classes of hearers and he spoke to Mangusri: "What, O Mangusri, is the cause, what is the reason of this wonderful, prodigious, miraculous shine having been produced by the Bhagavat? Look, how these eighteen thousand Buddha-fields appear variegated, extremely beautiful, directed by Tathagatas and superintended by Tathagatas."

Then it was that Maitreya, the Bodhisattva Mahasattva, addressed Mangusri, the prince royal, in the following stanzas:

1. Why, Mangusri, does this ray darted by the guide of men shine forth from between his brows? This single ray issuing from the circle of hair? And why this abundant rain of Mandaravas?

2. The gods, overjoyed, let drop Mangushakas and sandal powder, divine, fragrant, and delicious.

3. This earth is, on every side, replete with splendour, and all the four classes of the assembly are filled with delight, while the whole field shakes in six different ways, frightfully.

4. And that ray in the eastern quarter illuminates the whole of eighteen thousand Buddha-fields, simultaneously, so that those fields appear as gold-coloured.

5. The universe as far as the Aviki (hell) and the extreme limit of existence, with all beings of those fields living in any of the six states of existence, those who are leaving one state to be born in another;

6. Their various and different actions in those states have become visible; whether they are in a happy, unhappy, low, eminent, or intermediate position, all that I see from this place.

7. I see also the Buddhas, those lions of kings, revealing and showing the essence of the Dharma, comforting many kotis (astronomically large number) of creatures and emitting sweet-sounding voices.

8. They let go forth, each in his own field, a deep, sublime, wonderful voice, while proclaiming the Buddha-laws by means of myriads of kotis of illustrations and proofs.

9. And to the ignorant creatures who are oppressed with toils and distressed

in mind by birth and old age, they announce the bliss of Rest, saying: 'This is the end of trouble, O monks.'

10. And to those who are possessed of strength and vigour and who have acquired merit by virtue or earnest belief in the Buddhas, they show the vehicle of the Pratyekabuddhas, by observing this rule of the law.

11. And the other sons of the Buddha who, striving after superior knowledge, have constantly accomplished their various tasks, them also they admonish to enlightenment.

12. From this place, O Mangusri, I see and hear such things and thousands of kotis of other particulars besides; I will only describe some of them.

13. I see in many fields Bodhisattvas by many thousands of kotis, like sands of the Ganges, who are producing enlightenment according to the different degree of their power.

14. There are some who charitably bestow wealth, gold, silver, gold money, pearls, jewels, conch shells, stones, coral, male and female slaves, horses, and sheep;

15. As well as litters adorned with jewels. They are spending gifts with glad hearts, developing themselves for superior enlightenment, in the hope of gaining the vehicle.

16. Thus they think: 'The best and most excellent vehicle in the whole of the threefold world is the Buddha-vehicle magnified by the Buddhas. May I, forsooth, soon gain it after my spending such gifts.'

17. Some give carriages yoked with four horses and furnished with benches, flowers, banners, and flags; others give objects made of precious substances.

18. Some, again, give their children and wives; others their own flesh; or offer, when bidden, their hands and feet, striving to gain supreme enlightenment.

19. Some give their heads, others their eyes, others their dear own body, and after cheerfully bestowing their gifts they aspire to the knowledge of the Tathagatas.

20. Here and there, O Mangusri, I behold beings who have abandoned their flourishing kingdoms, harems, and continents, left all their counsellors and kinsmen,

21. And betaken themselves to the guides of the world to ask for the most excellent law, for the sake of bliss; they put on reddish-yellow robes, and shave hair and beard.

22. I see also many Bodhisattvas like monks, living in the forest, and others inhabiting the empty wilderness, engaged in reciting and reading.

23. And some Bodhisattvas I see, who full of wisdom betake themselves to mountain caves, where by cultivating and meditating the Buddha-knowledge they arrive at its perception.

24. Others who have renounced all sensual desires, by purifying their own self, have cleared their sphere and obtained the five transcendent faculties, live in the wilderness, as true sons of the Buddha.

25. Some are standing firm, the feet put together and the hands joined in token of respect towards the leaders, and are praising joyfully the king of the leading Jinas in thousands of stanzas.

26. Some thoughtful, meek, and tranquil, who have mastered the niceties of the course of duty, question the highest of men about the law, and retain in

their memory what they have learnt.

27. And I see here and there some sons of the principal Jina who, after completely developing their own self, are preaching the law to many kotis of living beings with many myriads of illustrations and reasons.

28. Joyfully they proclaim the law, rousing many Bodhisattvas; after conquering Mara, the Evil One, with his hosts and vehicles, they strike the drum of the Dharma.

29. I see some sons of the Buddha, humble, calm, and quiet in conduct, living under the command of the Buddhas, and honoured by men, gods, goblins, and Titans.

30. Others, again, who have retired to woody thickets, are saving the creatures in the hells by emitting radiance from their body, and rouse them to enlightenment.

31. There are some sons of the Jina who dwell in the forest, abiding in vigour, completely renouncing sloth, and actively engaged in walking; it is by energy that they are striving for supreme enlightenment.

32. Others complete their course by keeping a constant purity and an unbroken morality like precious stones and jewels; by morality do these strive for supreme enlightenment.

33. Some sons of the Jina, whose strength consists in forbearance, patiently endure abuse, censure, and threats from proud monks. They try to attain enlightenment by dint of forbearance.

34. Further, I see Bodhisattvas, who have forsaken all wanton pleasures, shun unwise companions and delight in having communication with genteel men.

35. Who, with avoidance of any distraction of thoughts and with attentive mind, during thousands of kotis of years have meditated in the caves of the wilderness; these strive for enlightenment by dint of meditation.

36. Some, again, offer in presence of the Jinas and the assemblage of disciples gifts consisting in food hard and soft, meat and drink, medicaments for the sick, in plenty and abundance.

37. Others offer in presence of the Jinas and the assemblage of disciples hundreds of kotis of clothes, worth thousands of kotis, and garments of priceless value.

38. They bestow in presence of the Buddhas hundreds of kotis of monasteries which they have caused to be built of precious substances and sandal-wood, and which are furnished with numerous lodgings.

39. Some present the leaders of men and their disciples with neat and lovely gardens abounding with fruits and beautiful flowers, to serve as places of daily recreation,

40. When they have, with joyful feelings, made such various and splendid donations, they rouse their energy in order to obtain enlightenment; these are those who try to reach supreme enlightenment by means of charitableness.

41. Others set forth the law of quietness, by many myriads of illustrations and proofs; they preach it to thousands of kotis of living beings; these are tending to supreme enlightenment by science.

42. There are sons of the Buddha who try to reach enlightenment by wisdom; they understand the law of indifference and avoid acting at the antinomy of things, unattached like birds in the sky.

43. Further, I see, O Mangusri, many Bodhisattvas who have displayed steadiness under the rule of the departed Buddhas, and now are worshipping the relics of the Jinas.

44. I see thousands of kotis of Stupas, numerous as the sand of the Ganges, which have been raised by these sons of the Jina and now adorn kotis of grounds.

45. Those magnificent Stupas, made of seven precious substances, with their thousands of kotis of umbrellas and banners, measure in height no less than 5000 yoganas and 2000 in circumference.

46. They are always decorated with flags; a multitude of bells is constantly heard sounding; men, gods, goblins, and Titans pay their worship with flowers, perfumes, and music.

47. Such honour do the sons of the Buddha render to the relics of the Jinas, so that all directions of space are brightened as by the celestial coral trees in full blossom.

48. From this spot I behold all this; those numerous kotis of creatures; both this world and heaven covered with flowers, owing to the single ray shot forth by the Jina.

49. O how powerful is the Bhagavat! How extensive and bright is his knowledge! that a single beam darted by him over the world renders visible so many thousands of fields!

50. We are astonished at seeing this sign and this wonder, so great, so incomprehensible. Explain me the matter, O Mangusri! The sons of Buddha are anxious to know it.

51. The four classes of the congregation in joyful expectation gaze on you, O Hero, and on me; gladden their hearts; remove their doubts; grant a revelation, O son of Buddha!

52. Why is it that the Buddha has now emitted such a light? O how great is the power of the Bhagavat! O how extensive and holy is his knowledge!

53. That one ray extending from him all over the world makes visible many thousands of fields. It must be for some purpose that this great ray has been emitted.

54. Is the Bhagavat to show the primordial laws which he, the Highest of men, discovered on the terrace of enlightenment? Or is he to prophesy the Bodhisattvas their future destiny?

55. There must be a weighty reason why so many thousands of fields have been rendered visible, variegated, splendid, and shining with gems, while Buddhas of infinite sight are appearing.

56. Maitreya asks the son of Jina; men, gods, goblins, and Titans, the four classes of the congregation, are eagerly awaiting what answer Mangusri shall give in explanation.

Whereupon Mangusri addressed Maitreya, the Bodhisattva Mahasattva, and the whole assembly of Bodhisattvas in these words: "It is the intention of the Tathagata, young men of good family, to begin a grand discourse for the teaching of the law, to pour the great rain of the Dharma, to make resound the great drum of the law, to raise the great banner of the law, to kindle the great torch of the law, to blow the great conch trumpet of the law, and to strike the great tymbal of the law. Again, it is the intention of the Tathagata, young men of good family, to make a grand exposition of the law this very day. Thus it appears to me, young men of good family, as I have witnessed a similar sign of the former Tathagatas, the Arhats, the perfectly enlightened. Those former Tathagatas, they, too, emitted a lustrous ray, and I am convinced that the Tathagata is about to deliver a grand discourse for the teaching of the Dharma and make his grand speech on the law everywhere heard, he having shown such a foretoken. And because the Tathagata, wishes that this Dharmaparyaya meeting opposition in all the world be heard everywhere, therefore does he display so great a miracle and this fore-token consisting in the lustre occasioned by the emission of a ray.

"I remember, young men of good family, that in the days of yore, many immeasurable, inconceivable, immense, infinite, countless Eons, more than countless Eons ago, nay, long and very long before, there was born a Tathagata called Kandrasuryapradipa, an Arhat, endowed with science and conduct, a Buddha, knower of the world, an incomparable tamer of men, a teacher and ruler of gods and men, a Buddha and Lord. He showed the Dharma; he revealed the duteous course which is holy at its commencement, holy in its middle, holy at the end, good in substance and form, complete and perfect, correct and pure. That is to say, to the disciples he preached the law containing the four Noble Truths, and starting from the chain of causes and effects, tending to overcome birth, decrepitude, sickness, death, sorrow, lamentation, woe, grief, despondency, and finally leading to Nirvana; and to the Bodhisattvas he preached the law connected with the six Perfections, and terminating in the knowledge of the Omniscient, after the attainment of supreme, perfect enlightenment.

"Now, young men of good family, long before the time of that Tathagata Kandrasuryapradipa, the Arhat, there had appeared a Tathagata, likewise called Kandrasuryapradipa, after whom, O Agita, there were twenty thousand Tathagatas, all of them bearing the name of Kandrasuryapradipa, of the same lineage and family name, to wit, of Bharadvaga. All those twenty thousand Tathagatas, O Agita, from the first to the last, showed the Dharma, revealed the course which is sacred at its commencement, sacred in its middle, sacred at the end.

"The aforesaid Lord Kandrasuryapradipa, the Tathagata, when a young prince and not yet having left home to embrace the ascetic life, had eight sons, the young princes: Sumati, Anantamati, Ratnamati, Viseshamati, Vimatisamudghatin, Ghoshamati, and Dharmamati. These eight young princes, Agita, sons to Bhagavat Kandrasuryapradipa, the Tathagata, had an immense fortune. Each of them was in possession of four great continents, where they exercised the kingly sway. When they saw that the Bhagavat had left his home to become an ascetic, and heard that he had attained supreme, perfect enlightenment, they forsook all of them the pleasures of royalty and followed the example of the Bhagavat by resigning the world; all of them strove to reach superior enlightenment and became preachers of the law. While constantly leading a holy life, those young princes planted roots of goodness under many thousands of Buddhas.

"It was at that time, Agita, that Bhagavat Kandrasuryapradipa, the Tathagata, after expounding the Dharmaparyaya called 'the Great Exposition,' a text of great extension, serving to instruct Bodhisattvas and proper to all Buddhas, at the same moment and instant, at the same gathering of the classes of hearers, sat cross-legged on the same seat of the law, and entered upon the meditation termed 'the Station of the exposition of Infinity.' His body was motionless, and his mind had reached perfect tranquillity. And as soon as Bhagavat had entered upon meditation, there fell a great rain of divine flowers, Mandaravas and great Mandaravas, Mangushakas and great Mangushakas, covering Bhagavat and the four classes of hearers, while the whole Buddha-fields shook in six ways; it moved, removed, trembled, trembled from one end to the other, tossed, tossed along.

"Then did those who were assembled and sitting together at that congregation, monks, nuns, male and fe-male lay devotees, gods, Nagas, goblins, Gandharvas, demons, Garudas, Kinnaras, great serpents, men and beings not human, as well as governors of a region, rulers of armies and rulers of four continents, all of them with their followers gaze on th Bhagavat in astonishment, in amazement, in ecstasy.

"And at that moment there issued a ray from within the circle of hair between the eyebrows of the Bhagavat. It extended over eighteen hundred thousand Buddha-fields in the eastern quarter, so that all those Buddha-fields appeared wholly illuminated by its radiance, just like the Buddha-fields do now, O Agita.

"At that juncture, O Agita, there were twenty kotis of Bodhisattvas following Bhagavat. All hearers of the Dharma in that assembly, on seeing how the world was illuminated by the lustre of that ray, felt astonishment, amazement, ecstasy, and curiosity.

"Now it happened, O Agita, that under the rule of the aforesaid Lord there was a Bodhisattva called Varaprabha, who had eight hundred pupils. It was to this Bodhisattva Varaprabha that Bhagavat, on rising from his meditation, revealed the Dharmaparyaya called 'the Lotus of the True Dharma (Law).' He spoke during fully sixty intermediate kalpas, always sitting on the same seat, with immovable body and tranquil mind. And the whole assembly continued sitting on the same seats, listening to the preaching of Bhagavat for sixty intermediate kalpas, there being not a single creature in that assembly who felt fatigue of body or mind.

"As Bhagavat Kandrasuryapradipa, the Tathagata, during sixty intermediate kalpas had been expounding the Dharmaparyaya called 'the Lotus of the True Dharma,' a text of great development, serving to instruct Bodhisattvas and proper to all Buddhas, he instantly announced his complete Nirvana to the world, including the gods, Maras and Brahmas, to all creatures, including ascetics, Brahmans, gods, men and demons, saying: Today, O monks, this very night, in the middle watch, will the Tathagata, by entering the element of absolute Nirvana, become wholly extinct.

"Thereupon, O Agita, Bhagavat Kandrasuryapradipa, the Tathigata, predestinated the Bodhisattva called Srigarbha to supreme, perfect

15

enlightenment, and then spoke thus to the whole assembly: 'O monks, this Bodhisattva Srigarbha here shall immediately after me attain supreme, perfect enlightenment, and become Vimalanetra, the Tathagata.'

"Thereafter, Agita, that very night, at that very watch, Bhagavat Kandrasuryapradipa, the Tathalgata, became extinct by entering the element of absolute Nirvana. And the aforementioned Dharmaparyaya, termed 'the Lotus of the True Dharma,' was kept in memory by the Bodhisattva Mahasattva Varaprabha; during eighty intermediate kalpas did the Bodhisattva Varaprabha keep and reveal the commandment of Bhagavat who had entered Nirvana. Now it so happened, O Agita, that the eight sons of Bhagavat Kandrasuryapradipa, Mati and the rest, were pupils to that very Bodhisattva Varaprabha. They were by him made ripe for supreme, perfect enlightenment, and in after times they saw and worshipped many hundred thousand myriads of kotis of Buddhas, all of whom had attained supreme, perfect enlightenment, the last of them being Dipankara, the Tathalgata.

"Amongst those eight pupils there was one Bodhisattva who attached an extreme value to gain, honour and praise, and was fond of glory, but all the words and letters one taught him faded from his memory, did not stick. So he got the appellation of Yasaskama. He had propitiated many hundred thousand myriads of kotis of Buddhas by that root of goodness, and afterwards esteemed, honoured, respected, revered, venerated, worshipped them. Perhaps, Agita, youfeelest some doubt, perplexity or misgiving that in those days, at that time, there was another Bodhisvattva Mahasattva Varaprabha, preacher of the Dharma. But do not think so. Why? because it is myself who in those days, at that time, was the Bodhisattva Mahasattva Varaprabha, preacher of the Dharma; and that Bodhisattva named Yasaskama, the lazy one, it is thyself, Agita, who in those days, at that time, wert the Bodhisattva named Yasaskama, the lazy one.

"And so, Agita, having once seen a similar foretoken of Bhagavat, I infer from a similar ray being emitted just now, that Bhagavat is about to expound the

Dharmaparyaya called 'the Lotus of the True Dharma.'"

And on that occasion, in order to treat the subject more copiously, Mangusri uttered the following verses:

57. I remember a past period, inconceivable, illimited kalpas ago, when the highest of beings, the Jina of the name of Kandrasuryapradipa, was in existence.

58. He preached the true Dharma, he, the leader of creatures; he educated an infinite number of kotis of beings, and roused inconceivably many Bodhisattvas to acquiring supreme Buddha-knowledge.

59. And the eight sons born to him, the leader, when he was prince royal, no sooner saw that the great sage had embraced ascetic life, than they resigned worldly pleasures and became monks.

60. And the Bhagavat of the world proclaimed the Dharma, and revealed to thousands of kotis of living beings the Sutra, the development, which by name is called 'the excellent Exposition of Infinity.'

61. Immediately after delivering his speech, the leader crossed his legs and entered upon the meditation of 'the excellent Exposition of the Infinite.' There on his seat of the law the eminent seer continued absorbed in meditation.

62. And there fell a celestial rain of Mandaravas, while the drums of heaven resounded without being struck; the gods and elves in the sky paid honour to the highest of men.

63. And simultaneously all the Buddha-fields began trembling. A wonder it was, a great prodigy. Then the chief emitted from between his brows one extremely beautiful ray,

64. Which moving to the eastern quarter glittered, illuminating the world all over the extent of eighteen thousand fields. It manifested the vanishing and appearing of beings.

65. Some of the fields then seemed jewelled, others showed the hue of lapis lazuli, all splendid, extremely beautiful, owing to the radiance of the ray from the leader.

66. Gods and men, as well as Nagas, goblins, Gandharvas, nymphs, Kinnaras, and those occupied with serving the Buddha became visible in the spheres and paid their devotion.

67. The Buddhas also, those self-born beings, appeared of their own accord, resembling golden columns; like unto a golden disk within lapis lazuli, they revealed the law in the midst of the assembly.

68. The disciples, indeed, are not to be counted, the disciples of Buddha are numberless. Yet the lustre of the ray renders them all visible in every field.

69. Energetic, without breach or flaw in their course, similar to gems and jewels, the sons of the leaders of men are visible in the mountain caves where they are dwelling.

70. Numerous Bodhisattvas, like the sand of the Ganges, who are spending all their wealth in giving alms, who have the strength of patience, are devoted to contemplation and wise, become all of them visible by that ray.

71. Immovable, unshaken, firm in patience, devoted to contemplation, and absorbed in meditation are seen the true sons of the Buddhas while they are striving for supreme enlightenment by dint of meditation.

72. They preach the Dharma in many spheres, and point to the true,

quiet, spotless state they know. Such is the effect produced by the power of the Buddha.

73. And all the four classes of hearers on seeing the power of the mighty Kandrarkadipa were filled with joy and asked one another: 'How is this?'

74. And soon afterwards, as the Leader of the world, worshipped by men, gods, and goblins, rose from his meditation, he addressed his son Varaprabha, the wise Bodhisattva and preacher of the law:

75. 'You are wise, the eye and refuge of the world; you are the trustworthy keeper of my law, and can not bear witness as to the treasure of laws which I am to lay bare to the good of living beings.'

76. Then, after rousing and stimulating, praising and lauding many Bodhisattvas, did the Jina proclaim the supreme laws during fully sixty intermediate kalpas.

77. And whatever excellent supreme law was proclaimed by the Bhagavat of the world while continuing sitting on the very same seat, was kept in memory by Varaprabha, the son of Jina, the preacher of the Dharma.

78. And after the Jina and Leader had manifested the supreme law and stimulated the numerous crowd, he spoke, that day, towards the world including the gods as follows:

79. 'I have manifested the rule of the Dharma; I have shown the nature of the law. Now, O monks, it is the time of my Nirvana; this very night, in the middle watch.

80. 'Be zealous and strong in persuasion; apply yourselves to my lessons; for the Jinas, the great seers, are but rarely met with in the lapse of myriads of kotis of Eons (kalpa, long period of time).'

81. The many sons of Buddha were struck with grief and filled with extreme sorrow when they heard the voice of the highest of men announcing that his Nirvana was near at hand.

82. To comfort so inconceivably many kotis of living beings the king of kings said: 'Be not afraid, O monks; after my Nirvana there shall be another Buddha.

83. 'The wise Bodhisattva Srigarbha, after finishing his course in faultless knowledge, shall reach highest, supreme enlightenment, and become a Jina under the name of Vimalagranetra.'

84. That very night, in the middle watch, he met complete extinction, like a lamp when the cause of its burning is exhausted. His relics were distributed, and of his Stupas there was an infinite number of myriads of kotis.

85. The monks and nuns at the time being, who strove after supreme, highest enlightenment, numerous as sand of the Ganges, applied themselves to the commandment of the Buddha.

86. And the monk who then was the preacher of the law and the keeper of the law, Varaprabha, expounded for fully eighty intermediate kalpas the highest laws according to the commandment of the Buddha.

87. He had eight hundred pupils, who all of them were by him brought to full development. They saw many kotis of Buddhas, great sages, whom they worshipped.

88. By following the regular course they became Buddhas in several spheres, and as they followed one another in immediate succession they successively foretold each other's future destiny to Buddhaship.

89. The last of these Buddhas following one another was Dipankara. He, the supreme god of gods, honoured by crowds of sages, educated thousands of kotis of living beings.

90. Among the pupils of Varaprabha, the son of Jina, at the time of his teaching the law, was one slothful, covetous, greedy of gain and cleverness.

91. He was also excessively desirous of glory, but very fickle, so that the lessons dictated to him and his own reading faded from his memory as soon as learnt.

92. His name was Yasaskama, by which he was known everywhere. By the accumulated merit of that good action, spotted as it was,

93. He propitiated thousands of kotis of Buddhas, whom he rendered ample honour. He went through the regular course of duties and saw the present Buddha Sakyasimha.

94. He shall be the last to reach superior enlightenment and become a Lord known by the family name of Maitreya, who shall educate thousands of kotis of creatures.

95. He who then, under the rule of the extinct Buddha, was so slothful, was thyself, and it was I who then was the preacher of the Dharma.

96. As on seeing a foretoken of this kind I recognise a sign such as I have seen manifested of yore, therefore and on that account I know,

97. That decidedly the chief of Jinas, the supreme king of the Sakyas, the All-seeing, who knows the highest truth, is about to pronounce the excellent Sutra which I have heard before.

98. That very sign displayed at present is a proof of the skilfulness of the leaders; the Lion of the Sakyas is to make an exhortation, to declare the fixed nature of the Dharma.

99. Be well prepared and well minded; join your hands: he who is affectionate and merciful to the world is going to speak, is going to pour the endless rain of the law and refresh those that are waiting for enlightenment.

100. And if some should feel doubt, uncertainty, or misgiving in any respect, then the Wise One shall remove it for his children, the Bodhisattvas here striving after enlightenment.

PART II.

SKILFULNESS

The Bhagavat then rose with recollection and consciousness from his meditation, and forthwith addressed the venerable Sariputra: "The Buddha knowledge, Sariputra, is profound, difficult to understand, difficult to comprehend. It is difficult for all disciples and Pratyekabuddhas to fathom the knowledge arrived at by the Tathagatas, and that, Sariputra, because the Tathagatas have worshipped many hundred thousand myriads of kotis of Buddhas; because they have fulfilled their course for supreme, complete enlightenment, during many hundred thousand myriads of kotis of Eons; because they have wandered far, displaying energy and possessed of wonderful and marvellous properties; possessed of properties difficult to understand; because they have found out things difficult to understand.

"The mystery of the Tathagatas, is difficult to understand, Sariputra, because when they explain the laws (or phenomena, things) that have their causes in themselves they do so by means of skilfulness, by the display of knowledge, by arguments, reasons, fundamental ideas, interpretations, and suggestions. By a variety of skilfulness they are able to release creatures that are attached to one point or another. The Tathagatas, Sariputra, have acquired the highest perfection in skilfulness and the display of knowledge; they are endowed with wonderful properties, such as the display of free and unchecked knowledge; the powers; the absence of hesitation; the independent conditions; the strength of the organs; the constituents of Bodhi; the contemplations; emancipations; meditations; the degrees of concentration of mind. The Tathagatas, Sariputra, are able to expound various things and have something wonderful and marvellous. Enough, Sariputra, let it suffice to say, that the Tathagatas, have something extremely wonderful, Sariputra. None but a Tathagatha, Sariputra, can impart to a Tathagata those laws which the Tathagata knows. And all laws, Sariputra, are taught by the Tathagata, and by him alone; no one but he knows all laws, what they are, how they are, like what they are, of what characteristics and of what nature they are."

And on that occasion, to set forth the same subject more copiously, the Bhagavat uttered the following stanzas:

1. Innumerable are the great heroes in the world that embraces gods and men; the totality of creatures is unable to completely know the leaders.

2. None can know their powers and states of emancipation, their absence of hesitation and Buddha properties, such as they are.

3. For a long time have I followed in presence of kotis of Buddhas the good course which is profound, subtle, difficult to understand, and most difficult to find.

4. After pursuing that career during an inconceivable number of kotis of Eons, I have on the terrace of enlightenment discovered the fruit thereof.

5. And therefore I recognise, like the other leaders of the world, how

23

THE LOTUS SUTRA OF THE TRUE DHARMA

it is, like what it is, and what are its characteristics.

6. It is impossible to explain it; it is unutterable; nor is there such a being in the world.

7. To whom this law could be explained or who would be able to understand it when explained, with the exception of the Bodhisattvas, those who are firm in resolve.

8. As to the disciples of the Knower of the world, those who have done their duty and received praise from the Buddhas, who are freed from faults and have arrived at the last stage of bodily existence, the Jina-knowledge lies beyond their sphere.

9. If this whole sphere were full of beings like Sariputra, and if they were to investigate with combined efforts, they would be unable to comprehend the knowledge of the Buddha.

10. Even if the ten points of space were full of sages like you, ay, if they were full of such as the rest of my disciples,

11. And if those beings combined were to investigate the knowledge of the Buddha, they would, all together, not be able to comprehend the Buddha-knowledge in its whole immensity.

12. If the ten points of space were filled with Pratyekabuddhas, free from faults, gifted with acute faculties, and standing in the last stage of their existence, as numerous as reeds and bamboos in Ganges, with undivided attention and subtle wit, even then that knowledge would be beyond their ken.

13. And if combined for an endless number of myriads of kotis of Eons, they were to investigate a part only of my superior laws, they would never find

out its real meaning.

14. If the ten points of space were full of Bodhisattvas who, after having don their duty under many kotis of Buddhas, investigated all things and preached many sermons, after entering a new vehicle;

15. If the whole world were full of them, as of dense reeds and bamboos, without any interstices, and if all combined were to investigate the law which the Buddha has realised;

16. If they were going on investigating for many kotis of Eons, as incalculable as the sand of the Ganges, with undivided attention and subtle wit, even then that knowledge would be beyond their understanding.

17. If such Bodhisattvas as are unable to fall back, numerous as the sand of the Ganges, were to investigate it with undivided attention, it would prove to lie beyond their ken.

18. Profound are the laws of the Buddhas, and subtle; all inscrutable and faultless. I myself know them as well as the Jinas do in the ten directions of the world.

19. O Sariputra, be full of trust in what the Buddha declares. The Jina speaks no falsehood, the great Seer who has so long preached the highest truth.

20. I address all disciples here, those who have set out to reach the enlightenment of Pratyekabuddhas, those who are roused to activity at my Nirvana, and those who have been released from the series of evils.

21. It is by my superior skilfulness that I explain the law at great length to the world at large. I deliver whosoever are attached to one point or another, and show the three vehicles.

The eminent disciples in the assembly headed by Agnata-Kaundinya, the twelve hundred Arhats faultless and self-controlled, the other monks, nuns, male and female lay devotees using the vehicle of disciples, and those who had entered the vehicle of Pratyeka-buddhas, all of them made this reflection: What may be the cause, what the reason of Bhagavat so extremely extolling the skilfulness of the Tathagatas? Of his extolling it by saying, 'Profound is the law by me discovered' of his extolling it by saying, 'It is difficult for all disciples and Pratyekabuddhas to understand it.' But as yet the Bhagavat has declared no more than one kind of emancipation, and therefore we also should acquire the Buddha-laws on reaching Nirvana. We do not catch the meaning of this utterance of the Bhagavat.

And the honorable Sariputra, who apprehended the doubt and uncertainty of the four classes of the audience and guessed their thoughts from what was passing in his own mind, himself being in doubt about the law, then said to the Bhagavat: "What, O Bhagavat, is the cause, what the reason of Bhagavat so repeatedly and extremely extolling the skilfulness, knowledge, and preaching of the Tathagata? Why does he repeatedly extol it by saying, 'Profound is the law by me discovered; it is difficult to understand the mystery of the Tathagatas.' Never before have I heard from Bhagavat such a discourse on the law. Those four classes of the audience, O Bhagavat, are overcome with doubt and perplexity. What is the Tathagata alluding to, when repeatedly extolling the profound law of the Tathagatas?"

On that occasion the venerable Sariputra uttered the following stanzas:

22. Now first does the Sun of men utter such a speech: 'I have acquired the powers, emancipations, and numberless meditations.'

23. And you mentioned the terrace of enlightenment without any one asking you. You mentioned the mystery, although no one asks you.

24. You spoke unasked and loudest in your own course. You mentioned that you have obtained knowledge and pronounced profound words.

25. Now a question rises in my mind and of these self-controlled, faultless beings striving after Nirvana - Why does the Jina speak in this manner?

26. Those who aspire to the enlightenment of Pratyekabuddhas, the nuns and monks, gods, Nagas, goblins, Gandharvas, and great serpents, are talking together, while looking up to the highest of men,

27. And ponder in perplexity. Give an elucidation, O Blessed One, to all the disciples of Buddha here assembled.

28. Myself have reached the perfection of virtue, have been taught by the supreme Sage; still, O highest of men! Even in my position I feel some doubt whether the course of duty shown to me shall receive its final sanction by Nirvana.

29. Let your voice be heard, O you whose voice resounds like an egregious kettle-drum! Proclaim your law such as it is. The legitimate sons of Jina here standing and gazing at the Jina, with joined hands;

30. As well as the gods, Nagas, goblins, Titans, numbering thousands of kotis, like sand of the of the Ganges; and those that aspire to superior enlightenment, here standing, fully eighty thousand in number.

31. Further, the kings, rulers of provinces and paramount monarchs, who have flocked thither from thousands of kotis of countries, are now standing with joined hands, and respectful, thinking: 'How are we to fulfil the course of duty?'

The venerable Sariputra having spoken, Bhagavat said to him: "Enough, Sariputra; it is of no use explaining this matter. Why? Because, Sariputra, the world, including the gods, would be frightened if this matter were expounded."

But the venerable Sariputra entreated Bhagavat a second time, saying: "Let Bhagavat expound, let the Buddha expound this matter, for in this assembly, O Bhagavat, there are many hundreds, many thousands, many hundred thousands, many hundred thousand myriads of kotis of living beings who have seen former Buddhas, who are intelligent, and will believe, value, and accept the words of Bhagavat."

The venerable Sariputra addressed Bhagavat with this stanza:

32. Speak clearly, O most eminent of Jinas! in this assembly there are thousands of living beings trustful, affectionate, and respectful towards the Buddha; they will understand the law by there expounded.

And Bhagavat said a second time to the venerable Sariputra: "Enough, Sariputra; it is of no use explaining this matter for the the world, including the gods, would be frightened if this matter were expounded, and some monks might be proud and come to a heavy fall."

And on that occasion uttered Bhagavat the following stanza:

32. Speak no more of it that I should declare this law! This knowledge is too subtle, inscrutable, and there are too many unwise men who in their conceit and foolishness would scoff at the law revealed."

A third time the venerable Sariputra entreated Bhagavat, saying: "Let Bhagavat expound, let the Buddha expound this matter. In this assembly, O Bhagavat, there are many hundreds of living beings my equals, and many hundreds, many thousands, many hundred thousands, many hundred thousand myriads of kotis of other living beings more, who in former births have been brought by Bhagavat to full ripeness. They will believe, value, and accept what Bhagavat declares, which shall tend to their advantage, weal, and happiness in length of time."

On that occasion the venerable Sariputra uttered the following stanzas:

34. Explain the law, O you the highest of men! I, your eldest son, beg you to do this. Here are thousands of kotis of beings who are to believe in the law revealed by you.

35. And those beings that in former births so long and constantly have by you been brought to full maturity and now are all standing here with joined hands, they, too, are to believe in this law.

36. Let the Buddha, seeing the twelve hundred, my equals, and those who are striving after superior enlightenment, speak to them and produce in them an extreme joy.

When Bhagavat for the third time heard the entreaty of the venerable Sariputra, he spoke to him as follows: "Now that you have asked the Tathagata a third time, Sariputra, I will answer you. Listen then, Sariputra, take well and duly to heart what I am saying; I am going to speak."

Now it happened that the five thousand proud monks, nuns and lay devotees of both sexes in the congregation rose from their seats and, after saluting to Bhagavat's feet, went to leave the assembly. Owing to the principle of good which there is in pride they imagined having attained what they had not, and having understood what they had not. Therefore, thinking themselves aggrieved, they went to leave the assembly, to which Bhagavat by his silence showed assent.

Thereupon Bhagavat addressed the venerable Sariputra: "My congregation, Sariputra, has been cleared from the chaff, freed from the trash; it is firmly established in the strength of faith. It is good, Sariputra, that those proud ones are gone away. Now I am going to expound the matter, Sariputra."

"Very well, O Bhagavat," replied the venerable Sariputra.

Bhagavat then began and said: "It is but now and then, Sariputra, that the Tathagata preaches such a discourse on the law as this. Just as but now and then is seen the blossom of the glomerous fig-tree, Sariputra, so does the Tathagata but now and then preach such a discourse on the law. Believe me, Sariputra, I speak what is real, I speak what is truthful, I speak what is right. It is difficult to understand the exposition of the mystery of the Tathagata, Sariputra; for in elucidating the law, Sariputra, I use hundred thousands of various skilful means, such as different interpretations, indications, explanations, illustrations. It is not by reasoning, Sariputra, that the law is to be found: it is beyond the pale of reasoning, and must be learnt from the Tathagata. For, Sariputra, it is for a sole object, a sole aim, verily a lofty object, a lofty aim that the Buddha, the Tathagata, appears in the world. And what is that sole object, that sole aim, that lofty object, that lofty aim of the Buddha, the Tathagata, appearing in the world? To show all creatures the sight of Tathagata-knowledge and to open the eyes of creatures for the sight of Tathagata-knowledge. This, O Sariputra, is the sole object, the sole aim, the sole purpose of his appearance in the world. Such then, Sariputra, is the sole object, the sole aim, the lofty object, the lofty aim of the Tathagata. And it is achieved by the Tathagata. For, Sariputra, I do show all creatures the sight of Tathagata-knowledge; I do open the eyes of creatures for the sight of Tathagata-knowledge, Sariputra; I do firmly establish the teaching of Tathagata-knowledge, Sariputra; I do lead the teaching of Tathagata-knowledge on the right path, Sariputra. By means of one sole vehicle, to wit, the Buddha-vehicle, Sariputra, do I teach creatures the law; there is no second vehicle, nor a third. This is the nature of the law, Sariputra, universally in the world, in all directions. For, Sariputra, all the Tathagatas, who in times past existed in countless, innumerable spheres in all directions for the good of many, the happiness of many, out of pity to the world, for the benefit, weal, and happiness of the great body of creatures, and who preached the law to gods and men with able means, such as several directions and indications, various arguments, reasons, illustrations, fundamental ideas, interpretations, paying regard to the dispositions of creatures whose inclinations and temperaments are so manifold, all those Buddhas and Lords, Sariputra, have preached the law to creatures by means of only one vehicle, the Buddha-vehicle, which finally leads to omniscience; it is identical with showing all creatures the sight of Tathagata-knowledge; with opening the eyes of creatures for the sight of Tathagata-knowledge; with the awakening by the display of Tathagata-knowledge; with leading the teaching of Tathagata-knowledge on the right path. Such is the law they have preached to creatures. And those creatures, Sariputra, who have heard the law from the past Tathagatas, have all of them reached supreme, perfect enlightenment.

"And the Tathagatas, who shall exist in future, Sariputra, in countless, innumerable spheres in all directions for the good of many, the happiness of many, out of pity to the world, for the benefit and happiness of the great body of creatures, and who shall preach the law to gods and men till the right path. Such is the law they shall preach to creatures. And those creatures, Sariputra, who shall hear the law from the future Tathagatas, shall all of them reach supreme, perfect enlightenment.

"And the Tathagatas, who now at present are staying, living, existing, Sariputra, in countless, innumerable spheres in all directions, and who are preaching the law to gods and men (as above till) the right path. Such is the law they are preaching to creatures. And those creatures, Sariputra, who are hearing the law from the present Tathagatas, shall all of them reach supreme, perfect enlightenment.

"I myself also, Sariputra, am at the present period a Tathagata, for the good of many till manifold; I myself also, Sariputra, am preaching the law to creatures till the right path. Such is the law I preach to creatures. And those creatures, Sariputra, who now are hearing the law from me, shall all of them

31

reach supreme, perfect enlightenment. In this sense, Sariputra, it must be understood that nowhere in the world a second vehicle is taught, far less a third.

"Yet, Sariputra, when the Tathagatas, happen to appear at the decay of the epoch, the decay of creatures, the decay of besetting sins, the decay of views, or the decay of lifetime; when they appear amid such signs of decay at the disturbance of the epoch; when creatures are much tainted, full of greed and poor in roots of goodness; then, Sariputra, the Tathagatas, use, skilfully, to designate that one and sole Buddha-vehicle by the appellation of the threefold vehicle. Now, Sariputra, such disciples, Arhats, or Pratyekabuddhaswho do not hear their actually being called to the Buddha-vehicle by the Tathagata, who do not perceive, nor heed it, those, Sariputra, should not be acknowledged as disciples of the Tathagata, nor as Arhats, nor as Pratyekabuddhas.

"Again, Sariputra, if there be some monk or nun pretending to Arhatship without an earnest vow to reach supreme, perfect enlightenment and saying, 'I am standing too high for the Buddha-vehicle, I am in my last appearance in the body before complete Nirvana,' then, Sariputra, consider such a one to be conceited. For, Sariputra, it is unfit, it is improper that a monk, a faultless Arhat, should not believe in the law which he hears from the Tathagata in his presence. I leave out of question when the Tathagata shall have reached complete Nirvana; for at that period, that time, Sariputra, when the Tathagata shall be wholly extinct, there shall be none who either knows by heart or preaches such Sutras as this. It will be under other Tathagatas, that they are to be freed from doubts. In respect to these things believe my words, Sariputra, value them, take them to heart; for there is no falsehood in the Tathagatas, Sariputra. There is but one vehicle, Sariputra, and that the Buddha-vehicle."

And on that occasion to set forth this matter more copiously Bhagavat uttered the following stanzas:

37. No less than five thousand monks, nuns, and lay devotees of both sexes, full of unbelief and conceit,

38. Remarking this slight, went, defective in training and foolish as they were, away in order to beware of damage.

39. Bhagavat, who knew them to be the dregs of the congregation, exclaimed: 'They have no sufficient merit to hear this law.'

40. My congregation is now pure, freed from chaff; the trash is removed and the pith only remains.

41. Hear from me, Sariputra, how this law has been discovered by the highest man, and how the mighty Buddhas are preaching it with many hundred proofs of skilfulness.

42. I know the disposition and conduct, the various inclinations of kotis of living beings in this world; I know their various actions and the good they have done before.

43. Those living beings I initiate in this law by the aid of manifold interpretations and reasons; and by hundreds of arguments and illustrations have I, in one way or another, gladdened all creatures.

44. I utter both Sutras and stanzas; legends, Gatakas, and prodigies, besides hundreds of introductions and curious parables.

45. I show Nirvana to the ignorant with low dispositions, who have followed no course of duty under many kotis of Buddhas, are bound to continued existence and wretched.

46. The self-born one uses such means to manifest Buddha-knowledge, but

he shall never say to them, you also are to become Buddhas.

47. Why should not the mighty one, after having waited for the right time, speak, now that he perceives the right moment is come? This is the fit opportunity of commencing the exposition of what really is.

48. Now the word of my commandment, as contained in nine divisions, has been published according to the varying degree of strength of creatures. Such is the device I have shown in order to introduce creatures to the knowledge of the giver of boons.

49. And to those in the world who have always been pure, wise, good-minded, compassionate sons of Buddha and done their duty under many kotis of Buddhas will I make known amplified Sutras.

50. For they are endowed with such gifts of mental disposition and such advantages of a blameless outward form that I can announce to them: in future you shall become Buddhas benevolent and compassionate.

51. Hearing which, all of them will be pervaded with delight at the thought: 'We shall become Buddhas pre-eminent in the world.' And I, perceiving their conduct, will again reveal amplified Sutras.

52. And those are the disciples of the Leader, who have listened to my word of command. One single stanza learnt or kept in memory suffices, no doubt of it, to lead all of them to enlightenment.

53. There is, indeed, but one vehicle; there is no second, nor a third anywhere in the world, apart from the case of the Purushottamas using an expedient to show that there is a diversity of vehicles.

54. The Leader of the world appears in the world to reveal the Buddha-knowledge. He has but one aim, indeed, no second; the Buddhas do not

bring over creatures by an inferior vehicle.

55. There where the self-born one has established himself, and where the object of knowledge is, of whatever form or kind; where the powers, the stages of meditation, the emancipations, the perfected faculties are; there the beings also shall be established.

56. I should be guilty of envy, should I, after reaching the spotless eminent state of enlightenment, establish any one in the inferior vehicle. That would not beseem me.

57. There is no envy whatever in me; no jealousy, no desire, nor passion. Therefore I am the Buddha, because the world follows my teaching.

58. When, splendidly marked with the thirty-two characteristics, I am illuminating this whole world, and, worshipped by many hundreds of beings, I show the unmistakable stamp of the nature of the law;

59. Then, Sariputra, I think thus: 'How will all beings by the thirty-two characteristics mark the self-born Seer, who of his own accord sheds his lustre all over the world?'

60. And while I am thinking and pondering, when my wish has been fulfilled and my vow accomplished I no more reveal Buddha-knowledge.

61. If, O son of Sari, I spoke to the creatures: 'Vivify in your minds the wish for enlightenment,' they would in their ignorance all go astray and never catch the meaning of my good words.

62. And considering them to be such, and that they have not accomplished their course of duty in previous existences, I see how they are attached and devoted to sensual pleasures, infatuated by desire and blind with delusion.

63. From lust they run into distress; they are tormented in the six states of existence and people the cemetery again and again; they are overwhelmed with misfortune, as they possess little virtue.

64. They are continually entangled in the thickets of sectarian theories, such as: 'It is and it is not; it is thus and it is not thus.' In trying to get a decided opinion on what is found in the sixty-two heretical theories they come to embrace falsehood and continue in it.

65. They are hard to correct, proud, hypocritical, crooked, malignant, ignorant, dull; hence they do not hear the good Buddha-call, not once in kotis of births.

66. To those, son of Sari, I show a device and say: 'Put an end to your trouble. When I perceive creatures vexed with mishap I make them see Nirvana.'

67. And so do I reveal all those laws that are ever holy and correct from the very first. And the son of -Buddha who has completed his course shall once be a Jina.

68. It is but my skilfulness which prompts me to manifest three vehicles; for there is but one vehicle and one track; there is also but one instruction by the leaders.

69. Remove all doubt and uncertainty; and should there be any who feel doubts, let them know that Bhagavats of the world speak the truth; this is the only vehicle, a second there is not.

70. The former Tathagatas also, living in the past for innumerable Eons, the many thousands of Buddhas who are gone to final rest, whose number can never be counted,

71. Those highest of men have all of them revealed most holy laws by means of illustrations, reasons, and arguments, with many hundred proofs of skilfulness.

72. And all of them have manifested but one vehicle and introduced but one on earth; by one vehicle have they led to full ripeness inconceivably many thousands of kotis of beings.

73. Yet the Jinas possess various and manifold means through which the Tathagata reveals to the world, including the gods, superior enlightenment, in consideration of the inclinations and dispositions of the different beings.

74. And all in the world who are hearing or have heard the law from the mouth of the Tathagatas, given alms, followed the moral precepts, and patiently accomplished the whole of their religious duties;

75. Who have acquitted themselves in point of zeal and meditation, with wisdom reflected on those laws, and performed several meritorious actions, have all of them reached enlightenment.

76. And such beings as were living patient, subdued, and disciplined, under the rule of the Jinas of those times, have all of them reached enlightenment.

77. Others also, who paid worship to the relics of the departed Jinas, erected many thousands of Stupas made of gems, gold, silver, or crystal,

78. Or built Stupas of emerald, cat's eye, pearls, egregious lapis lazuli, or sapphire; they have all of them reached enlightenment.

79. And those who erected Stupas from marble, sandal-wood, or eagle-wood; constructed Stupas from Deodar or a combination of different sorts of timber.

80. And who in gladness of heart built for the Jinas Stupas of bricks or clay; or caused mounds of earth to be raised in forests and wildernesses in dedication to the Jinas.

81. The little boys even, who in playing erected here and there heaps of sand with the intention of dedicating them as Stupas to the Jinas, they have all of them reached enlightenment.

82. Likewise have all who caused jewel images to be made and dedicated, adorned with the thirty-two characteristic signs, reached enlightenment.

83. Others who had images of Buddhas made of the seven precious substances, of copper or brass, have all of them reached enlightenment.

84. Those who ordered beautiful statues of Buddhas to be made of lead, iron, clay, or plaster have .

85. Those who made images of the Buddhas on painted walls, with complete limbs and the hundred holy signs, whether they drew them themselves or had them drawn by others.

86. Those even, whether men or boys, who during the lesson or in play, by way of amusement, made upon the walls such images with the nail or a piece of wood,

87. Have all of them reached enlightenment; they have become compassionate, and, by rousing many Bodhisattvas, have saved kotis of creatures.

88. Those who offered flowers and perfumes to the relics of the Tathagatas, to Stupas, a mound of earth, images of clay or drawn on a wall;

89. Who caused musical instruments, drums, conch trumpets, and noisy

great drums to be played, and raised the rattle of tymbals at such places in order to celebrate the highest enlightenment;

90. Who caused sweet lutes, cymbals, tabors, small drums, reed-pipes, flutes of ekonnada or sugar-cane to be made, have all of them reached enlightenment.

91. Those who to celebrate the Buddhas made thoughts, one shall in course of time see kotis of Buddhas.

92. They have all of them reached enlightenment. By paying various kinds of worship to the relics of the Buddhas, by doing but a little for the relics, by making resound were it but a single musical instrument;

93. Or by worshipping were it but with a single flower, by drawing on a wall the images of the Buddhas, by doing worship were it even with distracted thoughts, one shall in course of time see kotis of Buddhas.

94. Those who, when in presence of a Stupa, have offered their reverential salutation, be it in a complete form or by merely joining the hands; who, were it but for a single moment, bent their head or body;

95. And who at Stupas containing relics have one single time said: Homage be to Buddha! albeit they did it with distracted thoughts, all have attained superior enlightenment.

96. The creatures who in the days of those Buddhas, whether already extinct or still in existence, have heard no more than the name of the law, have all of them reached enlightenment.

97. Many kotis of future Buddhas beyond imagination and measure shall likewise reveal this device as Jinas and supreme Lords.

98. Endless shall be the skilfulness of these leaders of the world, by which they shall educate kotis of beings to that Buddha-knowledge which is free from imperfection.

99. Never has there been any being who, after hearing the law of those Leaders, shall not become Buddha; for this is the fixed vow of the Tathagatas: 'Let me, by accomplishing my course of duty, lead others to enlightenment.'

100. They are to expound in future days many thousand kotis of heads of the law; in their Tathagataship they shall teach the law by showing the sole vehicle before-mentioned.

101. The line of the law forms an unbroken continuity and the nature of its properties is always manifest. Knowing this, the Buddhas, the highest of men, shall reveal this single vehicle.

102. They shall reveal the stability of the law, its being subjected to fixed rules, its unshakeable perpetuity in the world, the awaking of the Buddhas on the elevated terrace of the earth, their skilfulness.

103. In all directions of space are standing Buddhas, like sand of the Ganges, honoured by gods and men; these also do, for the good of all beings in the world, expound superior enlightenment.

104. Those Buddhas while manifesting skilfulness display various vehicles though, at the same time, indicating the one single vehicle: the supreme place of blessed actions; with due regard to their strenuousness and vigour as well as their inclination, the Buddhas impart their lights to them.

105. Acquainted as they are with the conduct of all mortals, with their peculiar dispositions and previous actions; with due regard to their strenuousness and vigour, as well as their inclination, the Buddhas impart their lights to them.

106. By dint of knowledge the leaders produce many illustrations, arguments, and reasons; and considering how the creatures have various inclinations they impart various directions.

107. And myself also, the leader of the chief Jinas, am now manifesting, for the good of creatures now living, this Buddha enlightenment by thousands of kotis of various directions.

108. I reveal the Dharma in its multifariousness with regard to the inclinations and dispositions of creatures. I use different means to rouse each according to his own character. Such is the might of my knowledge.

109. I likewise see the poor wretches, deficient in wisdom and conduct, lapsed into the mundane whirl retained in dismal places, plunged in affliction incessantly renewed.

110. Fettered as they are by desire like the yak by its tail, continually blinded by sensual pleasure, they do not seek the Buddha, the mighty one; they do not seek the law that leads to the end of pain.

111. Staying in the six states of existence, they are benumbed in their senses, stick unmoved to the low views, and suffer pain on pain. For those I feel a great compassion.

112. On the terrace of enlightenment I have remained three weeks in full, searching and pondering on such a matter, steadily looking up to the tree there standing.

113. Keeping in view that king of trees with an unwavering gaze I walked round at its foot thinking: 'This law is wonderful and lofty, whereas creatures are blind with dulness and ignorance.'

114. Then it was that Brahma entreated me, and so did Indra, the four rulers of the cardinal points, Mahesvara, Isvara, and the hosts of Maruts by thousands of kotis.

115. All stood with joined hands and respectful, while myself was revolving the matter in my mind and thought: 'What shall I do? At the very time that I am uttering syllables, beings are oppressed with evils.'

116. In their ignorance they will not heed the law I announce, and in consequence of it they will incur some penalty. It would be better were I never to speak. May my quiet extinction take place this very day!

117. But on remembering the former Buddhas and their skilfulness, I thought: 'Nay, I also will manifest this tripartite Buddha-enlightenment.'

118. When I was thus meditating on the law, the other Buddhas in all the directions of space appeared to me in their own body and raised their voice, crying: 'Amen!

119. 'Amen, first Leader of the world! Now that you have come to unsurpassed knowledge, and are meditating on the skilfulness of the leaders of the world, you repeat their teaching.

120. 'We also, being Buddhas, will make clear the highest word, divided into three parts; for men occasionally have low inclinations, and might perchance from ignorance not believe us, when we say, you shall become Buddhas.

121. 'Hence we will rouse many Bodhisattvas by the display of skilfulness and the encouraging of the wish of obtaining fruits.'

122. And I was delighted to hear the sweet voice of the leaders of men; in the exultation of my heart I said to the blessed saints: 'The words of the eminent sages are not spoken in vain.

123. 'I, too, will act according to the indications of the wise leaders of the world; having myself been born in the midst of the degradation of creatures, I have known agitation in this dreadful world.'

124. When I had come to that conviction, O son of Sari, I instantly went to Benares, where I skilfully preached the Dharma to the five Solitaries, that law which is the base of final beatitude.

125. From that moment the wheel of my law has been moving, and the name of Nirvana made its appearance in the world, as well as the name of Arhat, of Dharma, and Sangha.

126. Many years have I preached and pointed to the stage of Nirvana, the end of wretchedness and mundane existence. Thus I used to speak at all times.

127. And when I saw, Sariputra, the children of the highest of men by many thousands of kotis, numberless, striving after the supreme, the highest enlightenment;

128. And when such as had heard the law of the Jinas, owing to the many-sidedness of their skilfulness, had approached me and stood before my face, all of them with joined hands, and respectful;

129. Then I conceived the idea that the time had come for me to announce the excellent law and to reveal supreme enlightenment, for which task I had been born in the world.

130. This event today will be hard to be understood by the ignorant who imagine they see here a sign, as they are proud and dull. But the Bodhisattvas, they will listen to me.

131. And I felt free from hesitation and highly cheered; putting aside all timidity, I began speaking in the assembly of the sons of Buddha, and roused them to enlightenment.

132. On beholding such worthy sons of Buddha I said: 'Your doubts also will be removed, and these twelve hundred disciples of mine, free from imperfections, all of them will become Buddhas.'

133. Even as the nature of the law of the former mighty saints and the future Jinas is, so is my law free from any doubtfulness, and it is such as I today preach it to you.

134. At certain times, at certain places, somehow do the leaders appear in the world, and after their appearance will they, whose view is boundless, at one time or another preach a similar law.

135. It is most difficult to meet with this superior law, even in myriads of kotis of Eons; very rare are the beings who will adhere to the superior law which they have heard from me.

136. Just as the blossom of the glomerous fig-tree is rare, albeit sometimes, at some places, and somehow it is met with, as something pleasant to see for everybody, as a wonder to the world including the gods;

137. So wonderful and far more wonderful is the law I proclaim. Any one who, on hearing a good exposition of it, shall cheerfully accept it and recite but one word of it, will have done honour to all Buddhas.

138. Give up all doubt and uncertainty in this respect; I declare that I am the king of the law (Dharmaraga); I am urging others to enlightenment, but I am here without disciples.

139. Let this mystery be for you, Sariputra, for all disciples of mine, and for

the eminent Bodhisattvas, who are to keep this mystery.

140. For the creatures, when at the period of the five depravities, are vile and bad; they are blinded by sensual desires, the fools, and never turn their minds to enlightenment.

141. Some beings, having heard this one and sole vehicle manifested by the Jina, will in days to come swerve from it, reject the Sutra, and go down to hell.

142. But those beings who shall be modest and pure, striving after the supreme and the highest enlightenment, to them shall I unhesitatingly set forth the endless forms of this one and sole vehicle.

143. Such is the mastership of the leaders, their skilfulness. They have spoken in many mysteries; hence it is difficult to understand them.

144. Therefore try to understand the mystery of the Buddhas, the holy masters of the world, forsake all doubt and uncertainty: you shall become Buddhas, rejoice!

PART III.

A PARABLE

Then the venerable Sariputra, pleased, glad, charmed, cheerful, thrilling with delight and joy, stretched his joined hands towards Bhagavat, and, looking up to Bhagavat with a steady gaze, addressed him in this strain: "I am astonished, amazed, O Bhagavat! I am in ecstasy to hear such a call from Bhagavat. For when, before I had heard of this law from Bhagavat, I saw other Bodhisattvas, and heard that the Bodhisattvas would in future get the name of Buddhas, I felt extremely sorry, extremely vexed to be, deprived from so grand a sight as the Tathagata-knowledge. And whenever, O Bhagavat, for my daily recreation I was visiting the caves of rocks or mountains, wood thickets, lovely gardens, rivers, and roots of trees, I always was occupied with the same and ever-recurring thought: 'Whereas the entrance into the fixed points (elements) of the law is nominally equal, we have been dismissed by Bhagavat with the inferior vehicle.' Instantly, however, O Bhagavat, I felt that it was our own fault, not Bhagavat's. For had we regarded Bhagavat at the time of his giving the all surpassing demonstration of the law, that is, the exposition of supreme, perfect enlightenment, then, O Bhagavat, we should have become adepts in those laws. But because, without understanding the mystery of Bhagavat, we, at the moment of the Bodhisattvas not being assembled, heard only in a hurry, caught, meditated, minded, took to heart the first lessons pronounced, therefore, O Bhagavat, I used to pass day and night in self-reproach. But today, O Bhagavat, I have reached complete extinction; today, O Bhagavat, I have become calm; today, O Bhagavat, I am wholly come to rest; today, O Bhagavat, I have reached Arhatship; today, O Bhagavat, I am Bhagavat's eldest son, born from his law, sprung into existence by the law, made by the law, inheriting from the law, accomplished by the law. My burning has left me, O Bhagavat, now that I have heard this wonderful law, which I had not leant before, announced by the voice from the mouth of Bhagavat."

And on that occasion the venerable Sariputra addressed Bhagavat in the following stanzas:

1. I am astonished, great Leader, I am charmed to hear this voice; I feel no doubt any more; now am I fully ripe for the superior vehicle.

2. Wonderful is the voice (call) of the Buddhas; it dispels the doubt and pain of living beings; my pain also is all gone now that I, freed from imperfections, have heard that voice.

3. When I was taking my daily recreation or was walking in woody thickets, when betaking myself to the roots of trees or to mountain caves, I indulged

in no other thought but this:

4. 'O how am I deluded by vain thoughts! Whereas the faultless laws are, nominally, equal, shall I in future not preach the superior law in the world?

5. 'The thirty-two characteristic signs have failed me, and the gold colour of the skin has vanished; all the ten powers and emancipations have likewise been lost. O how have I gone astray at the equal laws!

6. 'The secondary signs also of the great Seers, the eighty excellent specific signs, and the eighteen uncommon properties have failed me. O how am I deluded!'

7. And when I had perceived you, so benign and merciful to the world, and was lonely walking to take my daily recreation, I thought: 'I am excluded from that inconceivable, unbounded knowledge!'

8. Days and nights, O Bhagavat, I passed always thinking of the same subject; I would ask Bhagavat whether I had lost my rank or not.

9. In such reflections, O Chief of Jinas, I constantly passed my days and nights; and on seeing many other Bodhisattvas praised by the Leader of the world,

10. And on hearing this Buddha-law, I thought: 'To be sure, this is expounded mysteriously, it is an inscrutable, subtle, and faultless science, which is announced by the Jinas on the terrace of enlightenment'

11. Formerly I was attached to heretical theories, being a wandering monk and in high honour of the same opinions with the heretics; afterwards has Bhagavat, regarding my disposition, taught me Nirvana, to detach me from perverted views.

12. After having completely freed myself from all heretical views and reached the laws of void, I conceive that I have become extinct; yet this is not deemed to be extinction.

13. But when one becomes Buddha, a superior being, honoured by men, gods, goblins, Titans, and adorned with the thirty-two characteristic signs, then one will be completely extinct.

14. All those former cares have now been dispelled, since I have heard the voice. Now am I extinct, as you announced my destination before the world including the gods.

15. When I first heard the voice of Bhagavat, I had a great terror that it might be Mara, the Evil One, who on this occasion had adopted the disguise of Buddha.

16. But when the unsurpassed Buddha-wisdom had been displayed and established with arguments, reasons, and illustrations, by myriads of kotis, then I lost all doubt about the law I heard.

17. And when you had mentioned to me the thousands of kotis of Buddhas, the past Jinas who have come to final rest, and how they preached this law by firmly establishing it through skilfulness;

18. How the many future Buddhas and those who are now existing, as knowers of the real truth, shall expound or are expounding this law by hundreds of able devices;

19. And when you were mentioning your own course after leaving home, how the idea of the wheel of the law presented itself to your mind and how you decided upon preaching the law,

20. Then I was convinced: 'This is not Mara; it is Bhagavat of the world, who has shown the true course; no Maras can here abide.' So then my mind for a moment was overcome with perplexity,

21. But when the sweet, deep, and lovely voice of Buddha gladdened me, all doubts were scattered, my perplexity vanished, and I stood firm in knowledge.

22. I shall become a Tathagata, undoubtedly, worshipped in the world including the gods; I shall manifest Buddha-wisdom, mysteriously rousing many Bodhisattvas.

After this speech of the venerable Sariputra, Bhagavat said to him: "I declare to you, Sariputra, I announce to you, in presence of this world including the gods, Maras, and Brahmas, in presence of this people, including ascetics and Brahmans, that you, Sariputra, have been by me made ripe for supreme, perfect enlightenment, in presence of twenty hundred thousand myriads of kotis of Buddhas, and that you, Sariputra, have for a long time followed my commandments. You, Sariputra, are, by the counsel of the Bodhisattva, by the decree of the Bodhisattva, reborn here under my rule. Owing to the mighty will of the Bodhisattva, Sariputra, you have no recollection of your former vow to observe the religious course; of the counsel of the Bodhisattva, the decree of the Bodhisattva. You thought that you reached the final rest. Wishing to revive and renew in you the knowledge of your former vow to observe the religious course, I will now reveal to the disciples the Dharmaparyaya called the Lotus of the True Dharma.

"Again, Sariputra, at a future period, after innumerable, inconceivable, immeasurable Wons, when you will have learnt the true law of hundred thousand myriads of kotis of Tathagatas, showed devotion in various ways, and achieved the present Bodhisattva-course, you will become in the world a Tathagata, named Padmaprabha, endowed with science and conduct, a Buddha, a knower of the world, an unsurpassed tamer of men, a master of gods and men, a Buddha.

"At that time then, Sariputra, the Buddha-fields of Tathagata Padmaprabha is to be called Viraga and to be level, pleasant, delightful, extremely beautiful to see, pure, prosperous, rich, quiet, abounding with food, replete with many races of men; it will consist of lapis lazuli, and contain a checker-board of eight compartments distinguished by gold threads, each compartment having its jewel tree always and perpetually filled with blossoms and fruits of seven precious substances.

"Now that Tathagata Padmaprabha, Sariputra, will preach the Dharma by the instrumentality of three vehicles. Further, Sariputra, that Tathagata will not appear at the decay of the Eon, but preach the law by virtue of a vow.

"That Eon, Sariputra, will be named Maharatnapratimandita (Ornamented with magnificent jewels). Do you know, Sariputra, why that Eon is to be named Maharatnapratimandita? The Bodhisattvas of a Buddha-fields, Sariputra, are called ratnas (jewels), and at that time there will be many Bodhisattvas in that sphere called Viraga; innumerable, incalculable, beyond computation, abstraction made from their being computed by the Tathagatas. On that account is that Eon called Maharatnapratimandita.

"Now, to proceed, Sariputra, at that period the Bodhisattvas of that field will walking on jewel lotuses. And these Bodhisattvas will not be plying their work for the first time. They having accumulated roots of goodness observed the course of duty under many hundred thousand Buddhas; they are praised by the Tathagatas for their zealous application to Buddha-knowledge; are perfected in the rites preparatory to transcendent knowledge; accomplished in the direction of all true laws; mild and thoughtful. Generally, Sariputra, that Buddha-fields will teem with such Bodhisattvas.

"As to the lifetime, Sariputra, of that Tathagata Padmaprabha, it will last twelve intermediate kalpas, if we leave out of account the time of his being a young prince. And the lifetime of the creatures then living will measure eight intermediate kalpas. At the expiration of twelve intermediate kalpas, Sariputra, the Tathagata Padmaprabha, will announce the future destiny of the Bodhisattva called Dhritiparipurnan (Full of perseverance or endurance) that is to superior perfect enlightenment, to enter complete Nirvana: 'This Bodhisattva Mahasattva Dhritiparipurna shall immediately after me come to supreme, perfect enlightenment. He shall become in the world a Tathagata named Padmavrishabhavikramin, an Arhat, endowed with science and conduct.'

"Now the Tathagata Padmavrishabhavikramin, Sariputra, will have a Buddha-fields of quite the same description. The true law, Sariputra, of that Tathagata Padmavrishabhavikramin will, after his extinction, last thirty-two intermediate kalpas, and the counterfeit of his true law will last as many intermediate kalpas."

And on that occasion Bhagavat uttered the following stanzas:

23. You are, son of Sari, will in future be a Jina, a Tathagata named Padmaprabha, of unlimited sight; you will educate thousands of kotis of living beings.

24. After paying honour to many kotis of Buddhas, making strenuous efforts in the course of duty, and after having produced in thyself the ten powers, you will reach supreme, perfect enlightenment.

25. Within a period inconceivable and immense there shall be an Eon rich in jewels and a sphere named Viraga, the pure world of the highest of men;

26. And its ground will consist of lapis lazuli, and be set off with gold threads; it will have hundreds of jewel trees, very beautiful, and covered

with blossoms and fruits.

27. Bodhisattvas of good memory, able in showing the course of duty which they have been taught under hundreds of Buddhas, will come to be born in that field.

28. And the afore-mentioned Jina, then in his last bodily existence, shall, after passing the state of prince royal, renounce sensual pleasures, leave home to become a wandering ascetic, and thereafter reach the supreme and the highest enlightenment.

29. The lifetime of that Jina will be precisely twelve intermediate kalpas, and the life of men will then last eight intermediate kalpas.

30. After the extinction of the Tathagata the true law will continue thirty-two Eons in full, for the benefit of the world, including the gods.

31. When the true law shall have come to an end, its counterfeit will stand for thirty-two intermediate kalpas. The dispersed relics of the holy one will always be honoured by men and gods.

32. Such will be the fate of that Leader. Rejoice, O son of Sari, for it is you who will be that most excellent of men, so unsurpassed.

The four classes of the audience, monks, nuns, lay devotees male and female, gods, Nagas, goblins, Gandharvas, demons, Garudas, Kinnaras, great serpents, men and beings not human, on hearing this announcement of the venerable Sariputra's destiny to supreme, perfect enlightenment, were so pleased, glad, charmed, thrilling with delight and joy, that they covered Bhagavat severally with their own robes, while Indra the chief of gods, Brahma Sahampati, besides hundred thousands of kotis of other divine beings, covered him with heavenly garments and bestrewed him with flowers of heaven, Mandaravas and great Mandaravas. High aloft they whirled celestial clothes and struck hundred thousands of celestial musical instruments and cymbals, high in the sky; and after pouring a great rain of flowers they uttered these words: "The wheel of Dharma has been put in motion by Bhagavat. The first time at Benares at Rishipatana in the Deer-park; today has Bhagavat again put in motion the supreme wheel of the law."

And on that occasion those divine beings uttered the following stanzas:

33. The wheel of Dharma was put in motion by you, O you who is unrivalled in the world, at Benares, O great Hero! The wheel which rotates the rise and decay of all aggregates.

34. There it was put in motion for the first time; now, a second time, is it turned here. Today, O Bhavagat, you have preached this law, which is hard to be received with faith.

35. Many laws have we heard from Bhagavat of the world, but never before did we hear a law like this.

36. We receive with gratitude the mysterious speech of the great Sages, such as this prediction regarding Sariputra.

37. May we also become such incomparable Buddhas in the world, who by mysterious speech announce supreme Buddha-enlightenment.

38. May we also, by the good we have done in this world and in the next, and by our having propitiated the Buddha, be allowed to make a vow for Buddhaship.

Thereupon the venerable Sariputra thus spoke to Bhagavat: "My doubt is gone, O Bhagavat, my uncertainty is at an end on hearing from the mouth of Bhagavat my destiny to supreme enlightenment. But these twelve hundred self-controlled disciples, O Bhagavat, who have been placed by you on the stage of Saikshas, have been thus admonished and instructed: 'My preaching of the law, O monks, comes to this, that deliverance from birth, decrepitude, disease, and death is inseparably connected with Nirvana;' and these two thousand monks, O Bhagavat, your disciples, both those who are still under training and adepts, who all of them are free from false views about the soul, false views about existence, false views about cessation of existence, free from all false views, who are fancying themselves to have reached the stage of Nirvana, these have fallen into uncertainty by hearing from the mouth of Bhagavat this law which they had not heard before. Therefore, O Bhagavat, please speak to these monks, to dispel their uneasiness, so that the four classes of the audience, O Bhagavat, may be relieved from their doubt and perplexity."

On this speech of the venerable Sariputra Bhagavat said to him the following: "Have I not told you before, Sariputra, that the Tathagata, preaches the law by able devices, varying directions and indications, fundamental ideas, interpretations, with due regard to the different dispositions and inclinations of creatures whose temperaments are so various? All his preachings of the law have no other end but supreme and perfect enlightenment, for which he is rousing beings to the Bodhisattva-course. But, Sariputra, to elucidate this matter more at large, I will tell you a parable, for men of good understanding will generally readily enough catch the meaning of what is taught under the shape of a parable.

"Let us suppose the following case, Sariputra. In a certain village, town, borough, province, kingdom, or capital, there was a certain housekeeper, old, aged, decrepit, very advanced in years, rich, wealthy, opulent. He had a great house, high, spacious, built a long time ago and old, inhabited by some two, three, four, or five hundred living beings. The house had but one door, and a thatch; its terraces were tottering, the bases of its pillars rotten, the coverings and plaster of the walls loose. On a sudden the whole house was from every side put in conflagration by a mass of fire. Let us suppose that the man had many little boys, say five, or ten, or even twenty, and that he himself had come out of the house.

"Now, Sariputra, that man, on seeing the house from every side wrapt in a blaze by a great mass of fire, got afraid, frightened, anxious in his mind, and made the following reflection: 'I myself am able to come out from the burning house through the door, quickly and safely, without being touched or scorched by that great mass of fire; but my children, those young boys, are staying in the burning house, playing, amusing, and diverting themselves with all sorts of sports. They do not perceive, nor know, nor understand, nor mind that the house is on fire, and do not get afraid. Though scorched by that great mass of fire, and affected with such a mass of pain, they do not mind the pain, nor do they conceive the idea of escaping.'

"The man, Sariputra, is strong, has powerful arms, and so he makes this reflection: 'I am strong, and have powerful arms; why, let me gather all my little boys and take them to my breast to effect their escape from the house.' A second reflection then presented itself to his mind: 'This house has but one opening; the door is shut; and those boys, fickle, unsteady, and childlike as they are, will, it is to be feared, run hither and thither, and come to grief and disaster in this mass of fire. Therefore I will warn them.' So resolved, he calls to the boys: 'Come, my children! The house is burning with a mass of fire. Come, don't get burnt in that mass of fire'. But the ignorant boys do not heed the words of him who is their well-wisher; they are not afraid, not alarmed, and feel no misgiving; they do not care, nor fly, nor even know nor understand the purport of the word 'burning.' On the contrary, they run hither and thither, walk about, and repeatedly look at their father; all, because they are so ignorant.

"Then the man is going to reflect thus: 'The house is burning, is blazing by a mass of fire. It is to be feared that myself as well as my children will come to grief and disaster. Let me therefore by some skilful means get the boys out of the house'. The man knows the disposition of the boys, and has a clear perception of their inclinations. Now these boys happen to have many and manifold toys to play with, pretty, nice, pleasant, dear, amusing, and precious. The man, knowing the disposition of the boys, says to them: 'My children, your toys, which are so pretty, precious, and admirable, which you are so loth to miss, which are so various and multifarious, such as bullock-carts, goat-carts, deer-carts, which are so pretty, nice, dear, and precious to you, have all been put by me outside the house-door for you to play with. Come, run out, leave the house! To each of you I shall give what he wants. Come soon, come out for the sake of these toys'. And the boys, on hearing the names mentioned of such playthings as they like and desire, so agreeable to their taste, so pretty, dear, and delightful, quickly rush out from the burning house, with eager effort and great alacrity, one having no time to wait for the other, and pushing each other on with the cry of 'Who shall arrive first, the very first?'

"The man, seeing that his children have safely and happily escaped, and knowing that they are free from danger, goes and sits down in the open air on the square of the village, his heart filled with joy and delight, released from trouble and hindrance, quite at ease. The boys go up to the place where their father is sitting, and say: 'Father, give us those toys to play with, those bullock-carts, goat-carts, and deer-carts.' Then, Sariputra, the man gives to his sons, who run swift as the wind, bullock-carts only, made of seven precious substances, provided with benches, hung with a multitude of small bells, lofty, adorned with rare and wonderful jewels, embellished with jewel wreaths, decorated with garlands of flowers, carpeted with cotton mattresses and woollen coverlets, covered with white cloth and silk, having on both sides rosy cushions, yoked with white, very fair and fleet bullocks, led by a multitude of men. To each of his children he gives several bullockcarts of one appearance and one kind, provided with flags, and swift as the wind. That man does so, Sariputra, because being rich, wealthy, and in possession of many treasures and granaries, he rightly thinks: 'Why should I give these boys inferior carts, all these boys being my own children, dear and precious? I have got such great vehicles and ought to treat all the boys equally and without partiality. As I own many treasures and granaries, I could give such great vehicles to all beings, how much more than to my own children'. Meanwhile the boys are mounting the vehicles with feelings of astonishment and wonder. Now, Sariputra, what is your opinion? Has that man made himself guilty of a falsehood by first holding out to his children the prospect of three vehicles and afterwards giving to each of them the greatest vehicles, the most magnificent vehicles?"

Sariputra answered: "By no means, O Bhagavat, by no means, O Buddha. That is not sufficient to qualify the man as a speaker of falsehood, since it only was a skilful device to persuade his children to go out of the burning house and save their lives. Nay, besides recovering their very body, O Bhagavat, they have received all those toys. If that man, O Bhagavat, had given no single cart, even then he would not have been a speaker of falsehood, for he had previously been meditating on saving the little boys from a great mass of pain by some able device. Even in this case, O Bhagavat, the man would not have been guilty of falsehood, and far less now that he, considering his having plenty of treasures and prompted by no other motive but the love of his children, gives to all, to coax them, vehicles of one kind, and those the greatest vehicles. That man is not guilty of falsehood."

The venerable Siriputra having thus spoken, Bhagavat said to him: "Very well, very well, Sariputra, quite so; it is as you have said. So, too, Sariputra, the Tathagata, is free from all dangers, wholly exempt from all misfortune, despondency, calamity, pain, grief, the thick enveloping dark mists of ignorance. He, the Tathagata, endowed with Buddha-knowledge, forces, absence of hesitation, uncommon properties, and mighty by magical power, is the father of the world, who has reached the highest perfection in the knowledge of skilful means, who is most merciful, long-suffering, benevolent, compassionate. He appears in this triple world, which is like a house the roof and shelter whereof are decayed, a house burning by a mass of misery, in order to deliver from affection, hatred, and delusion the beings subject to birth, old age, disease, death, grief, wailing, pain, melancholy, despondency, the dark enveloping mists of ignorance, in order to rouse them to supreme and perfect enlightenment. Once born, he sees how the creatures are burnt, tormented, vexed, distressed by birth, old age, disease, death, grief, wailing, pain, melancholy, despondency; how for the sake of enjoyments, and prompted by sensual desires, they severally suffer various pains. In consequence both of what in this world they are seeking and what they have acquired, they will in a future state suffer various pains, in hell, in the brute creation, in the realm of Yama; they will suffer such pains as poverty in the world of gods or men, union with hateful persons or things, and separation from the beloved ones. And whilst incessantly whirling in that mass of evils they are sporting, playing, diverting themselves; they do not fear, nor dread, nor are they seized with terror; they do not know, nor mind; they are not startled, do not try to escape, but are enjoying themselves in that triple world which is like unto a burning house, and run hither and thither. Though overwhelmed by that mass of evil, they do not conceive the idea that they must beware of it.

"Under such circumstances, Sariputra, the Tathagata reflects thus: 'Verily, I am the father of these beings. I must save them from this mass of evil, and bestow on them the immense, inconceivable bliss of Buddha-knowledge, wherewith they shall sport, play, and divert themselves, wherein they shall find their rest.'

"Then, Sariputra, the Tathagata reflects thus: 'If, in the conviction of my possessing the power of knowledge and magical faculties, I manifest to these beings the knowledue, forces, and absence of hesitation of the Tathagata, without availing myself of some device, these beings will not escape. For they are attached to the pleasures of the five senses, to worldly pleasures; they will not be freed from birth, old age, disease, death, grief, wailing, pain, melancholy, despondency, by which they are burnt, tormented, vexed, distressed. Unless they are forced to leave the triple world which is like a house the shelter and roof whereof is in a blaze, how are they to get acquainted with Buddha-knowledge?'

"Now, Sariputra, even as that man with powerful arms, without using the strength of his arms, attracts his children out of the burning house by an able device, and afterwards gives them magnificent, great carts, so, Sariputra, the Tathagata, the Arhat, possessed of knowledge and freedom from all hesitation, without using them, in order to attract the creatures out of the triple world which is like a burning house with decayed roof and shelter, shows, by his knowledge of able devices, three vehicles, the vehicle of the disciples, the vehicle of the Pratyekabuddhas, and the vehicle of the Bodhisattvas. By means of these three vehicles he attracts the creatures and speaks to them thus: 'Do not delight in this triple world, which is like a burning house, in these miserable forms, sounds, odours, flavours, and contacts. For in delighting in this triple world ye are burnt, heated, inflamed with the thirst inseparable from the pleasures of the five senses. Fly from this triple world; betake yourselves to the three vehicles: the vehicle of the disciples, the vehicle of the Pratyekabuddhas, the vehicle of the Bodhisattvas. I give you my pledge for it, that I shall give you these three vehicles; make an effort to run out of this triple world.' And to attract them I say: 'These vehicles are grand, praised by the Aryas, and provided with most pleasant things; with such you are to sport, play, and divert yourselves in a noble manner. You will feel the great delight of the faculties, powers, constituents of Bodhi, meditations, the eight degrees of emancipation, self-concentration, and the results of self-concentration, and you will become greatly happy and cheerful.'

"Now, Sariputra, the beings who have become wise have faith in the Tathagata, the father of the world, and consequently apply themselves to his commandments. Among them there are some who, wishing to follow the dictate of an authoritative voice, apply themselves to the commandment of the Tathagata to acquire the knowledge of the four great truths, for the sake of their own complete Nirvana. These one may say to be those who, coveting the vehicle of the disciples, fly from the triple world, just as some of the boys will fly from that burning house, prompted by a desire of getting a cart yoked with deer. Other beings desirous of the science without a master, of self-restraint and tranquillity, apply themselves to the commandment of the Tathagata to learn to understand causes and effects, for the sake of their own complete Nirvana. These one may say to be those who, coveting the vehicle of the Pratyekabuddhas, fly from the triple world, just as some of the boys fly from the burning house, prompted by the desire of getting a cart yoked with goats. Others again desirous of the knowledge of the all-knowing, the knowledge of Buddha, the knowledge of the self-born one, the science without a master, apply themselves to the commandment of the Tathagata to learn to understand the knowledge, powers, and freedom from hesitation of the Tathagata, for the sake of the common good and happiness, out of compassion to the world, for the benefit, good, and happiness of the world at large, both gods and men, for the sake of the complete Nirvana of all beings. These one may say to be those who, coveting the great vehicle, fly from the triple world. Therefore they are called Bodhisattvas Mahasattvas. They may be likened to those among the boys who have fled from the burning house prompted by the desire of getting a cart yoked with bullocks.

"In the same manner, Sariputra, as that man, on seeing his children escaped from the burning house and knowing them safely and happily rescued and out of danger, in the consciousness of his great wealth, gives the boys one single grand cart; so, too, Sariputra, the Tathagata, the Arhat, on seeing many kotis of beings recovered from the triple world, released from sorrow, fear, terror, and calamity, having escaped owing to the command of the Tathagata, delivered from all fears, calamities, and difficulties, and having reached the bliss of Nirvana, so, too, Sariputra, the Tathagata, the Arhat, considering that he possesses great wealth of knowledge, power, and absence of hesitation, and that all beings are his children, leads them by no other vehicle but the Buddha-vehicle to full development. But he does not teach a particular Nirvana for each being; he causes all beings to reach complete Nirvana by means of the complete Nirvana of the Tathagata. And those beings, Sariputra, who are delivered from the triple world, to them the Tathagata gives as toys to amuse themselves with the lofty pleasures of the Aryas, the pleasures of meditation, emancipation, self-concentration, and its results; toys all of the same kind. Even as that man, Sariputra, cannot be said to have told a falsehood for having held out to those boys the prospect of three vehicles and given to all of them but one great vehicle, a magnificent vehicle made of seven precious substances, decorated with all sorts of ornaments, a vehicle of one kind, the most egregious of all, so, too, Sariputra, the Tathagata, the Arhat, tells no falsehood when by an able device he first holds forth three vehicles and afterwards leads all to complete Nirvana by the one great vehicle. For the Tathagata, Sariputra, who is rich in treasures and storehouses of abundant knowledge, powers, and absence of hesitation, is able to teach all beings the law which is connected with the knowledge of the all-knowing. In this way, Sariputra, one has to understand how the Tathagata by an able device and direction shows but one vehicle, the great vehicle."

And on that occasion Bhagavat uttered the following stanzas:

39. A man has an old house, large, but very infirm; its terraces are decaying and the columns rotten at their bases.

40. The windows and balconies are partly ruined, the wall as well as its coverings and plaster decaying; the coping shows rents from age; the thatch is everywhere pierced with holes.

41. It is inhabited by no less than five hundred beings; containing many cells and closets filled with excrements and disgusting.

42. Its roof-rafters are wholly ruined; the walls and partitions crumbling away; kotis of vultures nestle in it, as well as doves, owls, and other birds.

43. There are in every corner dreadful snakes, most venomous and horrible; scorpions and mice of all sorts; it is the abode of very wicked creatures of every description.

44. Further, one may meet there beings not belonging to the human race. It is defiled with excrement and urine, and teeming with worms, insects, and fire-flies; it resounds from the howling of dogs and jackals.

45. In it are horrible hyenas that devour human carcasses; many dogs and jackals greedily seeking the matter of corpses.

46. Those animals weak from perpetual hunger go about in several places to feed upon their prey and quarrelling fill the spot with their cries. Such is that most horrible house.

47. There are also very malign goblins, who violate human corpses; in several spots there are centipedes, huge snakes, and vipers.

48. Those animals creep into all corners, where they make nests to deposit their brood, which is often devoured by the goblins.

49. And when those cruel-minded goblins are satiated with feeding upon the flesh of other creatures, so that their bodies are big, then they commence sharply fighting on the spot.

50. In the wasted retreats are dreadful, malign urchins, some of them measuring one span, others one cubit or two cubits, all nimble in their movements.

51. They are in the habit of seizing dogs by the feet, throwing them upside down upon the floor, pinching their necks and using them ill.

52. There also live yelling ghosts naked, black, wan, tall, and high, who, hungry and in quest of food, are here and there emitting cries of distress.

53. Some have a mouth like a needle, others have a face like a cow's;

they are of the size of men or dogs, go with entangled hair, and utter plaintive cries from want of food.

54. Those goblins, ghosts, imps, like vultures, are always looking out through the windows and loopholes, in all directions in search of food.

55. Such is that dreadful house, spacious and high, but very infirm, full of holes, frail and dreary. Let us suppose that it is the property of a certain man,

56. And that while he is out of doors the house is reached by a conflagration, so that on a sudden it is wrapt in a blazing mass of fire on every side.

57. The beams and rafters consumed by the fire, the columns and partitions in flame are crackling most dreadfully, whilst goblins and ghosts are yelling.

58. Vultures are driven out by hundreds; urchins withdraw with parched faces; hundreds of mischievous beasts of prey I run, scorched, on every side, crying and shouting.

59. Many poor devils move about, burnt by the fire; while burning they tear one another with the teeth, and bespatter each other with their blood.

60. Hyenas also perish there, in the act of eating one another. The excrements burn, and a loathsome stench spreads in all directions.

61. The centipedes, trying to fly, are devoured by the urchins. The ghosts, with burning hair, hover about, equally vexed with hunger and heat.

62. In such a state is that awful house, where thousands of flames are breaking out on every side. But the man who is the master of the house looks on from without.

63. And he hears his own children, whose minds are engaged in playing with their toys, in their fondness of which they amuse themselves, as fools do in their ignorance.

64. And as he hears them he quickly steps in to save his children, lest his ignorant children might perish in the flames.

65. He tells them the defect of the house, and says: 'This is a miserable house, a dreadful one; the various creatures in it, and this fire to boot, form a series of evils.

66. 'In it are snakes, mischievous goblins, urchins, and ghosts in great number; hyenas, troops of dogs and jackals, as well as vultures, seeking their prey.

67. 'Such beings live in this house, which, apart from the fire, is extremely dreadful, and miserable enough; and now comes to it this fire blazing on all sides.'

68. The foolish boys, however, though admonished, do not mind their father's words, deluded as they are by their toys; they do not even understand him.

69. Then the man thinks: 'I am now in anxiety on account of my children. What is the use of my having sons if I lose them? No, they shall not perish by this fire.'

70. Instantly a device occurred to his mind: 'These young children are fond of toys, and have none just now to play with. Oh, they are so foolish!'

71. He then says to them: 'Listen, my sons, I have carts of different sorts, yoked with deer, goats, and excellent bullocks, lofty, great, and completely furnished.

72. 'They are outside the house; run out, do with them what you like; for your sake have I caused them to be made. Run out all together, and rejoice to have them!'

73. All the boys, on hearing of such carts, exert themselves, immediately rush out hastily, and reach, free from harm, the open air.

74. On seeing that the children have come out, the man betakes himself to the square in the centre of the village, and there from the throne he is sitting on he says: 'Good people, now I feel at ease.

75. 'These poor sons of mine, whom I have recovered with difficulty, my own dear twenty young children, were in a dreadful, wretched, horrible house, full of many animals.

76. 'As it was burning and wrapt in thousands of flames, they were amusing themselves in it with playing, but now I have rescued them all. Therefore I now feel most happy.'

77. The children, seeing their father happy, approached him and said: 'Dear father, give us those nice vehicles of three kinds, as you have promised;

78. 'And make true all that you promised us in the house. Do give them; it is now the right time.'

79. Now the man as we have supposed had a mighty treasure of gold, silver, precious stones, and pearls; he possessed bullion, numerous slaves, domestics, and vehicles of various kinds;

80. Carts made of precious substances, yoked with bullocks, most excellent, with benches and a row of tinkling bells, decorated with umbrellas and flags, and adorned with a network of gems and pearls.

81. They are embellished with gold, and artificial wreaths hanging down here and there; covered all around with excellent cloth and fine white muslin.

82. Those carts are moreover furnished with choice mattresses of fine silk, serving for cushions, and covered with choice carpets showing the images of cranes and swans, and worth thousands of kotis.

83. The carts are yoked with white bullocks, well fed, strong, of great size, very fine, who are tended by numerous persons.

84. Such excellent carts that man gives to all his sons, who, overjoyed and charmed, go and play with them in all directions.

85. In the same manner, Sariputra, I, the great Seer, am the protector and father of all beings, and all creatures who, childlike, are captivated by the pleasures of the triple world, are my sons.

86. This triple world is as dreadful as that house, overwhelmed with a number of evils, entirely inflamed on every side by a hundred different sorts of birth, old age, and disease.

87. But I, who am detached from the triple world and serene, am living in absolute retirement in a wood. This triple world is my domain, and those who in it are suffering from burning heat are my sons.

88. And I told its evils because I had resolved upon saving them, but they would not listen to me, because all of them were ignorant and their hearts attached to the pleasures of sense.

89. Then I employ an able device, and tell them of the three vehicles, so showing them the means of evading the numerous evils of the triple world which are known to me.

90. And those of my sons who adhere to me, who are mighty in the six transcendent faculties (abhignas) and the triple science, the Pratyekabuddhas, as well as the Bodhisattvas unable to slide back;

91. And those others who equally are my sons, to them I just now am showing, by means of this excellent allegory, the single Buddha-vehicle. Receive it; you shall all become Jinas.

92. It is most excellent and sweet, the most exalted in the world, that knowledge of the Buddhas, the most high among men; it is something sublime and adorable.

93. The powers, meditations, degrees of emancipation and self-concentration by many hundreds of kotis, that is the exalted vehicle in which the sons of Buddha take a never-ending delight.

94. In playing with it they pass days and nights, fortnights, months, seasons, years, intermediate kalpas, nay, thousands of kotis of kalpas.

95. This is the lofty vehicle of jewels which sundry Bodhisattvas and the disciples listening to the Buddha employ to go and sport on the terrace of enlightenment.

96. Know then that there is no second vehicle in this world anywhere to be found, in whatever direction you shall search, apart from the device shown by the most high among men.

97. You are my children, I am your father, who has removed you from pain, from the triple world, from fear and danger, when you had been burning for many kotis of Eons.

98. And I am teaching blessed rest (Nirvana) and though you have not

yet reached final rest, you are delivered from the trouble of the mundane whirl, provided you seek the vehicle of the Buddhas.

99. Any Bodhisattvas here present obey my Buddha-rules. Such is the skilfulness of the Jina that he disciplines many Bodhisattvas.

100. When the creatures in this world delight in low and contemptible pleasures, then the Leader of the world, who always speaks the truth, indicates pain as the first great truth.

101. And to those who are ignorant and too simple-minded to discover the root of that pain I lay open the way: 'Awaking of full consciousness, strong desire is the origin of pain.'

102. Always try, unattached, to suppress desire. This is my third truth, that of suppression. It is an infallible means of deliverance; for by practising this method one shall become emancipated.

103. And from what are they emancipated, Sariputra? They are emancipated from chimeras. Yet they are not wholly freed; the Leader declares that they have not yet reached final rest in this world.

104. Why is it that I do not pronounce one to be delivered before one's having reached the highest, supreme enlightenment? Because such is my will; I am the ruler of the law, who is born in this world to lead to beatitude.

105. This, Sariputra, is the closing word of my law which now at the last time I pronounce for the good of the world including the gods. Preach it in all quarters.

106. And if someone speaks to you these words: 'I joyfully accept,' and with signs of utmost reverence receives this Sutra, you may consider that man to be unable to slide back.

107. To believe in this Sutra one must have seen former Tathagatas, paid honour to them, and heard a law similar to this.

108. To believe in my supreme word one must have seen me; you and the assembly of monks have seen all these Bodhisattvas.

109. This Sutra is apt to puzzle the ignorant, and I do not pronounce it before having penetrated to superior knowledge. Indeed, it is not within the range of the disciples, nor do the Pratyekabuddhas come to it.

110. But you, Sariputra, have good will, not to speak of my other disciples here. They will walk in my faith, though each cannot have his individual knowledge.

111. But do not speak of this matter to haughty persons, nor to conceited ones, nor to Yogins who are not self-restrained; for the fools, always revelling in sensual pleasures, might in their blindness scorn the law manifested.

112. Now hear the dire results when one scorns my skilfulness and the Buddha-rule for ever fixed in the world; when one, with sullen brow, scorns the vehicle.

113. Hear the destiny of those who have scorned such a Sutra like this, whether during my lifetime or after my Nirvana, or who have wronged the monks.

114. After having disappeared from among men, they shall dwell in the lowest hell (Aviki) during a whole kalpa, and thereafter they shall fall lower and lower, the fools, passing through repeated births for many intermediate kalpas.

115. And when they have vanished from among the inhabitants of hell, they

shall further descend to the condition of brutes, be even as dogs and jackals, and become a sport to others.

116. Under such circumstances they shall grow blackish of colour, spotted, covered with sores, itchy; moreover, they shall be hairless and feeble, all those who have an aversion to my supreme enlightenment.

117. They are ever despised among animals; hit by clods or weapons they yell; everywhere they are threatened with sticks, and their bodies are emaciated from hunger and thirst.

118. Sometimes they become camels or asses, carrying loads, and are beaten with whips and sticks; they are constantly occupied with thoughts of eating, the fools who have scorned the Buddha-rule.

119. At other times they become ugly jackals, half blind and crippled; the helpless creatures are vexed by the village boys, who throw clods and weapons at them.

120. Again shooting off from that place, those fools become animals with bodies of five hundred yoganas, whirling round, dull and lazy.

121. They have no feet, and creep on the belly; to be devoured by many kotis of animals is the dreadful punishment they have to suffer for having scorned a Sutra like this.

122. And whenever they assume a human shape, they are born crippled, maimed, crooked, one-eyed, blind, dull, and low, they having no faith in my Sutra.

123. Nobody keeps their side; a putrid smell is continually issuing from their mouths; an evil spirit has entered the body of those who do not believe in this supreme enlightenment.

124. Needy, obliged to do menial labour, always in another's service, feeble, and subject to many diseases they go about in the world, unprotected.

125. The man whom they happen to serve is unwilling to give them much, and what he gives is soon lost. Such is the fruit of sinfulness.

126. Even the best-prepared medicaments, administered to them by able men, do, under those circumstances, but increase their illness, and the disease has no end.

127. Some commit thefts, affrays, assaults, or acts of hostility, whereas others commit robberies of goods; all this befalls the sinner.

128. Never does he behold Bhagavat of the world, the King of kings ruling the earth, for he is doomed to live at a wrong time, he who scorns my Buddha-rule.

129. Nor does that foolish person listen to the law; he is deaf and senseless; he never finds rest, because he has scorned this enlightenment.

130. During many hundred thousand myriads of kotis of Eons equal to the sand of the Ganges he shall be dull and defective; that is the evil result from scorning this Sutra.

131. Hell is his garden (or monastery), a place of misfortune his abode; he is continually living amongst asses, hogs, jackals, and dogs.

132. And when he has assumed a human shape he is to be blind, deaf, and stupid, the servant of another, and always poor.

133. Diseases, myriads of kotis of wounds on the body, scab, itch, scurf, leprosy, blotch, a foul smell are, in that condition, his covering and apparel.

134. His sight is dim to distinguish the real. His anger appears mighty in him, and his passion is most violent; he always delights in animal wombs.

135. Were I to go on, Sariputra, for a whole Eon, enumerating the evils of him who shall scorn my Sutra, I should not come to an end.

136. And since I am fully aware of it, I command you, Sariputra, that you shall not expound a Sutra like this before foolish people.

137. But those who are sensible, instructed, thoughtful, clever, and learned, who strive after the highest supreme enlightenment, to them expound its real meaning.

138. Those who have seen many kotis of Buddhas, planted immeasurably many roots of goodness, and undertaken a strong vow, to them expound its real meaning.

139. Those who, full of energy and ever kindhearted, have a long time been developing the feeling of kindness, have given up body and life, in their presence you may preach this Sutra.

140. Those who show mutual love and respect, keep no communication with ignorant people, and are content to live in mountain caverns, to them expound this hallowed Sutra.

141. If you see sons of Buddha who attach themselves to virtuous friends and avoid bad friends, then reveal to them this Sutra.

142. Those sons of Buddha who have not broken the moral vows, are pure like gems and jewels, and devoted to the study of the great Sutras, before those you may propound this Sutra.

143. Those who are not irascible, ever sincere, full of compassion for all living beings, and respectful towards the Buddha, before those you may propound this Sutra.

144. To one who in the congregation, without any hesitation and distraction of mind, speaks to expound the law, with many myriads of kotis of illustrations, you may manifest this Sutra

145. And he who, desirous of acquiring all-knowingness, respectfully lifts his joined hands to his head, or who seeks in all directions to find some monk of sacred eloquence;

146. And he who keeps in memory the great Ritras, while he never shows any liking for other books, nor even knows a single stanza from another work; to all of them you may expound this sublime Sutra.

147. He who seeks such an excellent Sutra as this, and after obtaining it devoutly worships it, is like the man who wears a relic of the Tathagata he has eagerly sought for.

148. Never mind other Satras nor other books in which a profane philosophy is taught; such books are fit for the foolish; avoid them and preach this Sutra.

149. During a full Eon, Sariputra, I could speak of thousands of kotis of connected points, but this suffices - you may reveal this Sutra to all who are striving after the highest supreme enlightenment

PART IV.

DISPOSITION

As the venerable Subhuti, the venerable MahaKatyayana, the venerable Maha-Kasyapa, and the venerable Maha-Maudgalyayana heard this law unheard of before, and as from the mouth of Bhagavat they heard the future destiny of Sariputra to superior perfect enlightenment, they were struck with wonder, amazement, and rapture. They instantly rose from their seats and went up to the place where Bhagavat was sitting; after throwing their cloak over one shoulder, fixing the right knee on the ground and lifting up their joined hands before Bhagavat, looking up to him, their bodies bent, bent down and inclined, they addressed Bhagavat in this strain:

"O Bhagavat, we are old, aged, advanced in years, honoured as seniors in this assemblage of monks. Worn out by old age we fancy that we have attained Nirvana; we make no efforts, O Bhagavat, for supreme perfect enlightenment; our force and exertion are inadequate to it. Though Bhagavat preaches the law and has long continued sitting, and though we have attended to that preaching of the law, yet, O Bhagavat, as we have so long been sitting and so long attended Bhagavat's service, our greater and minor members, as well as the joints and articulations, begin to ache. Hence, O Bhagavat, we are unable, in spite of Bhagavat's preaching, to realise the fact that all is vanity (or void), purposeless, and unfixed; we have conceived no longing after the Buddha-laws, the divisions of the Buddha-fields, the sports [or display of magical phenomena] of the Bodhisattvas or Tathagatas. For by having fled out of the triple world, O Bhagavat, we imagined having attained Nirvana, and we are decrepit from old age. Hence, O Bhagavat, though we have exhorted other Bodhisattvas and instructed them in supreme perfect enlightenment, we have in doing so never conceived a single thought of longing. And just now, O Bhagavat, we are hearing from Bhagavat that disciples also may be predestined to supreme perfect enlightenment. We are astonished and amazed, and deem it a great that today, on a sudden, we have heard from Bhagavat a voice (call) such as we never heard before. We have

74

acquired a magnificent jewel, O Bhagavat, an incomparable jewel. We had not sought, nor searched, nor expected, nor required so magnificent a jewel. It has become clear to us, O Bhagavat; it has become clear to us, O Buddha.

"It is a case, O Bhagavat, as if a certain man went away from his father and betook himself to some other place. He lives there in foreign parts for many years, twenty or thirty or forty or fifty. In course of time the one (the father) becomes a great man; the other (the son) is poor; in seeking a livelihood for the sake of food and clothing he roams in all directions and goes to some place, whereas his father removes to another country. The latter has much wealth, gold, corn, treasures, and granaries; possesses much gold and silver, many gems, pearls, lapis lazuli, conch shells, and stone, corals, gold and silver; many slaves male and female, servants for menial work. and journeymen; is rich in elephants, horses, carriages, cows, and sheep. He keeps a large retinue; has his money invested in great territories, and does great things in business, money-lending, agriculture, and commerce.

"In course of time, O Bhagavat, that poor man, in quest of food and clothing, roaming through villages, towns, boroughs, provinces, kingdoms, and royal capitals, reaches the place where his father, the owner of much wealth and gold, treasures and granaries, is residing. Now the poor man's father, the owner of much wealth and gold, treasures and granaries, who was residing in that town, had always and ever been thinking of the son he had lost fifty years ago, but he gave no utterance to his thoughts before others, and was only pining in himself and thinking: 'I am old, aged, advanced in years, and possess abundance of bullion, gold, money and corn, treasures and granaries, but have no son. It is to be feared lest death shall overtake me and all this perish unused.' Repeatedly he was thinking of that son: 'O how happy should I be, were my son to enjoy this mass of wealth!'

"Meanwhile, O Bhagavat, the poor man in search of food and clothing was gradually approaching the house of the rich man, the owner of abundant bullion, gold, money and corn, treasures and granaries. And the father of the poor man happened to sit at the door of his house, surrounded and waited upon by a great crowd of Brahmans, Kshatriyas, Vaisyas, and Sudras; he was sitting on a magnificent throne with a footstool decorated with gold and silver, while dealing with hundred thousands of kotis of gold-pieces, and fanned with a chowrie, on a spot under an extended awning inlaid with pearls and flowers and adorned with hanging garlands of jewels; sitting in great pomp. The poor man saw his own father in such pomp sitting at the door of the house, surrounded with a great crowd of people and doing a householder's business. The poor man frightened, terrified, alarmed, seized with a feeling of horripilation all over the body, and agitated in mind, reflects thus: 'Unexpectedly have I here fallen in with a king or grandee. People like me have nothing to do here; let me go; in the street of the poor I am likely to find food and clothing without much difficulty. Let me no longer tarry at this place, lest I be taken to do forced labour or incur some other injury.'

"Thereupon, O Bhagavat, the poor man quickly departs, runs off, does not tarry from fear of a series of supposed dangers. But the rich man, sitting on the throne at the door of his mansion, has recognised his son at first sight, in consequence whereof he is content, in high spirits, charmed, delighted, filled with joy and cheerfulness. He thinks: 'Wonderful! He who is to enjoy this plenty of bullion, gold, money and corn, treasures and granaries, has been found! He of whom I have been thinking again and again, is here now that I am old, aged, advanced in years.'

"At the same time, moment, and instant, O Bhagavat, he despatches couriers, to whom he says: 'Go and quickly fetch me that man.' The fellows thereon all run forth in full speed and overtake the poor man, who, frightened, terrified, alarmed, seized with a feeling of horripilation all over his body, agitated in mind, utters a lamentable cry of distress, screams, and exclaims: 'I have given you no offence.' But the fellows drag the poor man, however lamenting, violently with them. He, frightened, terrified, alarmed, seized with a feeling of horripilation all over his body, and agitated in mind, thinks by himself: 'I fear lest I shall be punished with capital punishment; I am lost.' He faints away, and falls on the earth. His father dismayed and near despondency says to those fellows: 'Do not carry the man in that manner.' With these words he sprinkles him with cold water without addressing him any further. For that householder knows the poor man's humble disposition I and his own elevated position; yet he feels that the man is his son.

"The householder, O Bhagavat, skilfully conceals from every one that it is his son. He calls one of his servants and says to him: 'Go and tell that poor man that he is free.' The servant obeys, approaches the poor man and tells him: 'Go, you are free.' The poor man is astonished and amazed at hearing these words; he leaves that spot and wanders to the street of the poor in search of food and clothing. In order to attract him the householder develops a method. He employs for it two men ill-favoured and of little splendour. He says: 'Go to the man you saw in this place; hire him in your own name for a double daily fee, and order him to do work here in my house. And if he asks: What - work shall I have to do? Tell him: Help us in clearing the heap of dirt.' The two fellows go and seek the poor man and engage him for such work as mentioned. Thereupon the two fellows conjointly with the poor man clear the heap of dirt in the house for the daily pay they receive from the rich man, while they take up their abode in a hovel of straw in the neighbourhood of the rich man's dwelling. And that rich man beholds through a window his own son clearing the heap of dirt, at which sight he is anew struck with wonder and astonishment.

"Then the householder descends from his mansion, lays off his wreath and ornaments, parts with his soft, clean, and gorgeous attire, puts on dirty raiment, takes a basket in his right hand, smears his body with dust, and goes to his son, whom he greets from afar, and thus addresses: 'Please, take the baskets and without delay remove the dust.' In this way he manages to speak to his son, to have a talk with him and say: 'Do remain here in my service, do not go again to another place. I will give you extra pay and whatever you want. You can confidently ask me got anything, be it the price of a pot, a smaller pot, a boiler or wood, or be it the price of salt, food, or clothing. I have got an old cloak; if you want it, ask me for it and I will give it to you. Any utensil of such sort, when you want to have it, I will give it you. Be at ease, fellow. Look upon me as if I were your father, for I am older and you are younger and you have rendered me much service by clearing this heap of dirt. As long as you have been in my service you have never shown any wickedness, crookedness, arrogance, or hypocrisy. I have discovered in you no vice at all of such as are commonly seen in other servants. From henceforward you are like my own son to me.

"From that time, the householder addresses the poor man by the name as his son, and the latter feels in presence of the householder as a son to his father. In this manner the householder affected with longing for his son employs him for the clearing of the heap of dirt during twenty years, at the end of which the poor man feels quite at ease in the mansion to go in and out, though he continues taking his abode in the hovel of straw.

"After a while the householder falls sick and feels that the time of his death is near. He says to the poor man: 'I possess abundant bullion, gold, money and corn, treasures and granaries. I am very sick and wish to have one upon whom to bestow my wealth; by whom it is to be received, and with whom it is to be deposited. Accept it. For in the same manner as I am the owner of it, so are you; you will not suffer anything of it to be wasted.

"And so the poor man accepts the abundant bullion, gold, money and corn, treasures and granaries of the rich man, but for himself he is quite indifferent to it and requires nothing from it. He continues living in the same hovel of straw and considers himself as poor as before.

"After a while the householder perceives that his son is able to save, mature and mentally developed, that in the consciousness of his nobility he feels abashed, ashamed, disousted, when thinking of his former poverty. When the time of his death approaching, the householder sends for the poor man, presents him to a gathering of his relations, before the king in the presence of citizens and country-people, and makes the following speech: 'Hear this! This is my own son, by me begotten. It is now fifty years that he disappeared from such and such a town. He is called so and so and myself I am called so and so. In searching after him I have come here from that town. He is my son and I am his father. To him I leave all my revenues and all my personal wealth shall he acknowledge his own.'

"The poor man hearing this speech was astonished and amazed; he thought by himself: 'Unexpectedly have I obtained this bullion, gold, money and corn, treasures and granaries.'

"Even so, O Bhagavat, do we represent the sons of the Tathagata, and the Tathagata says to us: 'You are my sons as the householder did. We were oppressed, O Bhagavat, with three difficulties: the difficulty of pain, the difficulty of conceptions, the difficulty of transition (or evolution); and in the worldly whirl we were disposed to what is low. Then have we been prompted by Bhagavat to ponder on the numerous inferior conditions that are similar to a heap of dirt. Once directed to them we have been practising, making efforts, and seeking for nothing but Nirvana as our fee. We were content, O Bhagavat, with the Nirvana obtained and thought to have gained much at the hands of the Tathagata because of we applied ourselves to these laws, practised, and made efforts. But Bhagavat takes no notice of us, does not mix with us, nor tell us that this treasure of the Tathagata's knowledge shall belong to us, though Bhagavat skilfully appoints us as heirs to this treasure of the knowledge of the Tathagata. And we, O Bhagavat, are not impatiently longing to enjoy it, because we deem it a great gain already to receive from Bhagavat Nirvana as our fee. We preach to the Bodhisattvas Mahasattvas a sublime sermon about the knowledge of the Tathagata; we explain, show, demonstrate the knowledge of the Tathagata, O Bhagavat, without longing. For the Tathagata by his skilfulness knows our disposition, whereas we ourselves do not know, nor apprehend. It is for this very reason that Bhagavat just now tells us that we are to him as sons, and that he reminds us of being heirs to the Tathagata. For the case stands thus: we are as sons to the Tathagata, but low of disposition. Bhagavat perceives the strength of our disposition and applies to us the denomination of Bodhisattvas. We are, however, charged with a double office in so far as in presence of Bodhisattvas we are called persons of low disposition and at the same time have to rouse them to Buddha-enlightenment. Knowing the strength of our disposition Bhagavat has thus spoken, and in this way, O Bhagavat, do we say that we have obtained unexpectedly and without longing the jewel of omniscience, which we did not desire, nor seek, nor search after, nor expect, nor require; and that inasmuch as we are the sons of the Tathagata."

On that occasion the venerable Maha-Kasyapa uttered the following stanzas:

1. We are stricken with wonder, amazement, and rapture at hearing a voice (call). It is the lovely voice, the Leader's voice, that so unexpectedly we hear today.

2. In a short moment we have acquired a great heap of precious jewels such as we were not thinking of, nor requiring. All of us are astonished to hear it.

3. It is like the history of a young, person who, seduced by foolish people, went away from his father and wandered to another country far distant.

4. The father was sorry to perceive that his son had run away and in his sorrow roamed the country in all directions during no less than fifty years.

5. In search of his son he came to some great city, where he built a house and dwelt, blessed with all that can gratify the five senses.

6. He had plenty of bullion and gold, money and corn, conch shells and coral, elephants, horses and servants, cows, cattle, and sheep.

7. Interests, revenues, properties, male and female slaves and a great number of servants, was highly honoured by thousands of kotis and a constant favourite of the king's.

8. The citizens bow to him with joined hands, as well as the villagers in the rural districts, many merchants come to him, and persons charged with numerous affairs.

9. In such way the man becomes wealthy, but he gets old, aged, advanced in years, and he passes days and nights always sorrowful in mind on account of his son.

10. He thinks: 'It is fifty years since that foolish son has run away. I have got plenty of wealth and the hour of my death draws near.'

11. Meanwhile that foolish son is wandering from village to village, poor and miserable, seeking food and clothing.

12. When begging, he at one time gets something, another time he does not. He grows lean in his travels, the unwise boy, while his body is vitiated with scabs and itch.

13. In course of time he in his rovings reaches the town where his father is living, and comes to his father's mansion to beg for food and raiment.

14. And the wealthy man happens to sit at the door on a throne under a canopy expanded in the sky and surrounded with many hundreds of living beings.

15. His trustees stand round him, some of them counting money and bullion, some writing bills, some lending money on interest.

16. The poor man, seeing the splendid mansion of the householder, thinks

within himself: 'Where am I? This man must be a king or a grandee.'

17. 'Let me not incur some injury and be caught to do forced labour.' With these reflections he hurried away inquiring after the road to the street of the poor.

18. The rich man on the throne is glad to see his own son and despatches messengers with the order to fetch that poor man.

19. The messengers immediately seize the man, but he is no sooner caught than he faints away as he thinks: 'These are certainly executioners who have approached me. What do I want clothing or food?'

20. On seeing it, the wealthy man thinks: 'This foolish person is of low disposition and will have no faith in my magnificence, nor believe that I am his father.'

21. Under those circumstances he orders persons of low character, crooked, one-eyed, maimed, ill-clad, to go and search that man who shall do menial work.

22. His message becomes: 'Enter my service and cleanse the putrid heap of dirt, replete with faeces and urine; I will give you a double salary.'

23. On hearing this call the poor man comes and cleanses the said spot; he takes up his abode there in a hovel near the mansion.

24. The rich man continually observes him through the windows and thinks: 'There is my son engaged in a low occupation, cleansing the heap of dirt.'

25. Then he descends, takes a basket, puts on dirty garments, and goes near the man. He chides him, saying: 'You do not perform your work.'

26. If you perform better, I will give you double salary and twice more ointment for the feet. I will give you food with salt, potherbs, and a cloak.

27. So he chides him at the time, but afterwards he wisely conciliates him by saying: 'You do your work very well, indeed; you are my son. Surely, there is no doubt of it.'

28. Little by little he makes the man enter the house and employs him in his service for fully twenty years, in the course of which time he succeeds in inspiring him with confidence.

29. At the same time he lays up in the house gold, pearls, and crystal, draws up the sum total and is always occupied in his mind with all that property.

30. The ignorant man, who is living outside the mansion alone in a hovel, cherishes no other ideas but of poverty and thinks to himself: 'Mine are no such possessions!'

31. The rich man perceiving this of him thinks: 'My son has arrived at the consciousness of being noble.' He calls together a gathering of his friends and relatives and says: 'I will give all my property to this man.'

32. In the midst of the assembly where the king, burghers, citizens, and many merchantmen were present, he speaks thus: 'This is my son whom I lost a long time ago.

33. 'It is now fully fifty years-and twenty years more during which I have seen him-that he disappeared from such and such a place and that in his search I came to this place.'

34. 'He is owner of all my property; to him I leave it all and entirely;

let him do with it what he wants; I give him my whole family property.'

35. And the poor man is struck with surprise; remembering his former poverty, his low disposition, and as he receives those good things of his father's and the family property, he thinks: 'Now I am a happy man.'

36. In like manner has the Leader, who knows of our low disposition, not declared to us: 'You shall become Buddhas,' but declared, 'You are, certainly, my disciples and sons.'

37. And Bhagavat of the world enjoins us: 'Teach, Kasyapa, the superior path to those that strive to attain the highest summit of enlightenment, the path by following which they are to become Buddhas.'

38. Being thus ordered by the Buddha, we show the path to many Bodhisattvas of great might, by means of myriads of kotis of illustrations and proofs.

39. And by hearing us the sons of Jina realise that eminent path to attain enlightenment, and in that case receive the prediction that they are to become Buddhas in this world.

40. Such is the work we are doing strenuously, preserving this law-treasure and revealing it to the sons of Jina, in the manner of that man who had deserved the confidence of that other man.

41. Yet, though we diffuse the Buddha-treasure we feel ourselves to be poor; we do not require the knowledge of the Jina, and yet, at the same time, we reveal it.

42. We fancy an individual (separate) Nirvana. So far, no further does our knowledge reach; nor do we ever rejoice at hearing of the divisions of Buddha-fields.

43. All these laws are faultless, unshaken, exempt from destruction and commencement; but there is no law in them. When we hear this, however, we cannot believe.

44. We have put aside all aspiration to superior Buddha-knowledge a long time ago; never have we devoted ourselves to it. This is the last and decisive word spoken by the Jina.

45. In this bodily existence, closing with Nirvana, we have continually accustomed our thoughts to the void. We have been released from the evils of the triple world we were suffering from and have accomplished the command of the Jina.

46. To whomsoever among the sons of Jina who in this world are on the road to superior enlightenment we revealed the law, and whatever law we taught, we never had any predilection for it.

47. And the Master of the world, the Self-born one, takes no notice of us, waiting his time. He does not explain the real connection of the things, as he is testing our disposition.

48. Able in applying devices at the right time, like that rich man he says: 'Be constant in subduing your low disposition,' and to those who are subdued he gives his wealth.

49. It is a very difficult task which Bhagavat of the world is performing, a task in which he displays his skilfulness, when he tames his sons of low disposition and thereupon imparts to them his knowledge.

50. On a sudden have we today been seized with surprise, just as the poor man who acquired riches; now for the first time have we obtained the fruit under the rule of Buddha, a fruit as excellent as faultless.

51. As we have always observed the moral precepts under the rule of the Knower of the world, we now receive the fruit of that morality which we have formerly practised.

52. Now have we obtained the egregious, hallowed, exalted, and perfect fruit of our having observed an excellent and pure spiritual life under the rule of the Leader.

53. Now, O Bhagavat, are we disciples, and we shall proclaim supreme enlightenment everywhere, reveal the word of enlightenment, by which we are formidable disciples.

54. Now have we become Arhats, O Bhagavat; and deserving of the worship of the world, including the gods, Maras and Brahmas, in short, of all beings.

55. Who is there, even were he to exert himself during kotis of Eons, able to thwart you, who accomplishes in this world of mortals such difficult things as those, and others even more difficult I?

56. It would be difficult to offer resistance with hands, feet, head, shoulder, or breast, even were one to try during as many complete Eons as there are grains of sand in the Ganges.

57. One may charitably give food, soft and solid, clothing, drink, a place for sleeping and sitting, with clean coverlets; one may build monasteries of sandal-wood, and after furnishing them with double pieces of fine white muslin, present them;

58. One may be assiduous in giving medicines of various kinds to the sick, in honour of the Buddha; one may spend alms during as many Eons as there are grains of sand in the Ganges-even then one will not be able to offer resistance.

59. Of sublime nature, unequalled power, miraculous might, firm in the strength of patience is the Buddha; a great ruler is the Jina, free from imperfections. The ignorant cannot bear or understand such things as these.

60. Always returning, he preaches the law to those whose course of life is conditioned, he, Bhagavat of the law, Bhagavat of all the world, the great Lord, the Chief among the leaders of the world.

61. Fully aware of the circumstances or places of all beings he indicates their duties, so multifarious, and considering the variety of their dispositions he inculcates the law with thousands of arguments.

62. He, the Tathagata, who is fully aware of the course of all beings and individuals, preaches a multifarious law, while pointing to this superior enlightenment."

PART V.

ON PLANTS

Thereupon Bhagavat addressed the venerable Maha-Kasyapa and the other senior great disciples, and said: "Very well, very well, Kasyapa. You have done very well to proclaim the real qualities of the Tathagata. They are the real qualities of the Tathagata, Kasyapa, but he has many more, innumerable, incalculable, the end of which it would be difficult to reach, even were one to continue enumerating them for immeasurable Eons. The Tathagata, Kasyapa, is the master of the law, the king, lord, and master of all laws. And whatever law for any case has been instituted by the Tathagata, remains unchanged. All laws, Kasyapa, have been aptly instituted by the Tathagata. In his Tathagata-wisdom he has instituted them in such a manner that all those laws finally lead to the stage of those who know all. The Tathagata also distinctly knows the meaning of all laws. The Tathagata is possessed of the faculty of penetrating all laws, possessed of the highest perfection of knowledge, so that he is able to decide all laws, able to display the knowledge of the allknowing, impart the knowledge of the all-knowing, and lay down the rules of the knowledge of the all-knowing.

"It is a case, Kasyapa, similar to that of a great cloud big with rain, coming up in this wide universe over all grasses, shrubs, herbs, trees of various species and kind, families of plants of different names growing on earth, on hills, or in mountain caves, a cloud covering the wide universe to pour down its rain everywhere and at the same time. Then, Kasyapa, the grasses, shrubs, herbs, and wild trees in this universe, such as have young and tender stalks, twigs, leaves, and foliage, and such as have middle-sized stalks, twigs, leaves, and foliage, and such as have the same fully developed, all those grasses, shrubs, herbs, and wild trees, smaller and greater other trees will each, according to its faculty and power, suck the humid element from the water emitted by that great cloud, and by that water which, all of one essence, has been abundantly poured down by the cloud, they will each, according to its germ, acquire a regular development, growth, shooting up, and bigness; and so they will produce blossoms and fruits, and will receive, each severally, their names. Rooted in one and the same soil, all those families of plants and germs are drenched and vivified by water of one essence throughout.

"In the same manner, Kasyapa, does the Tathagata appear in the world. Like unto a great cloud coming up, the Tathagata appears and sends forth his call to the whole world, including gods, men, and demons. And even as a great cloud, Kasyapa, extending over the whole universe, in like manner, Kasyapa, the Tathagata before the face of the world, including gods, men, and demons, lifts his voice and utters these words: 'I am the Tathagata, O gods and men! The Arhat, the perfectly enlightened one; having reached the shore myself, I carry others to the shore; being free, I make free; being comforted, I comfort; being perfectly at rest, I lead others to rest. By my perfect wisdom I know both this world and the next, such as they really are. I am all-knowing, all-seeing. Come to me, O gods and men! Hear the law. I am he who indicates the path; who shows the path, as knowing the path, being acquainted with the path.' Then, Kasyapa, many hundred thousand myriads of kotis of beings come to hear the law of the Tathagata; and the Tathagata, who knows the difference as to the faculties and the energy of those beings, produces various Dharmaparyayas, tells many tales, amusing, agreeable, both instructive and pleasant, tales by means of which all beings not only become pleased with the law in this present life, but also after death will reach happy states, where they are to enjoy many pleasures and hear the law. By listening to the law they will be freed from hindrances and in due course apply themselves to the law of the all-knowing, according to their faculty, power, and strength.

"Even as the great cloud, Kasyapa, after expanding over the whole universe, pours out the same water and recreates by it all grasses, shrubs, herbs, and trees; even as all these grasses, shrubs, herbs, and trees, according to their faculty, power, and strength, suck in the water and thereby attain the full development assigned to their kind; in like manner, Kasyapa, is the law preached by the Tathagata, the Arhat, of one and the same essence, that is to say, the essence of it is deliverance, the final aim being absence of passion, annihilation, knowledge of the all-knowing. As to that, Kasyapa, it must be understood that the beings who hear the law when it is preached by the Tathagata, who keep it in their memory and apply themselves to it, do not know, nor perceive, nor understand their own self. For, Kasyapa, the Tathagata only really knows who, how, and of what kind those beings are; what, how, and whereby they are meditating; what, how, and whereby they are contemplating; what, why, and whereby they are attaining. No one but the Tathagata, Kasyapa, is there present, seeing all intuitively, and seeing the state of those beings in different stages, as of the lowest, highest, and mean grasses, shrubs, herbs, and trees. I am he, Kasyapa, who, knowing the law which is of but one essence - the essence of deliverance, the law ever peaceful, ending in Nirvana, the law of eternal rest - having but one stage and placed in voidness, who knowing this does not on a sudden reveal to all the knowledge of the all-knowing, since I pay regard to the dispositions of all beings.

"You are astonished, Kasyapa, that you cannot fathom the mystery expounded by the Tathagata. It is, Kasyapa, because the mystery expounded by the Tathagatas, the Arhats, is difficult to be understood."

And on that occasion, the more fully to explain the same subject, Bhagavat uttered the following stanzas:

1. I am the Dharmaraga, born in the world as the destroyer of existence. I declare the law to all beings after discriminating their dispositions.

2. Superior men of wise understanding guard the word, guard the mystery, and do not reveal it to living beings.

3. That science is difficult to be understood; the simple, if hearing it on a sudden, would be perplexed; they would in their ignorance fall out of the way and go astray.

4. I speak according to their reach and faculty; by means of various meanings I accommodate my view.

5. It is, Kasyapa, as if a cloud rising above the horizon shrouds all space in darkness and covers the earth.

6. That great rain-cloud big with water, is wreathed with flashes of lightning and rouses with its thundering call all creatures.

7. By warding off the sunbeams, it cools the region; and gradually lowering so as to come in reach of hands, it begins pouring down its water all around.

8. And so, flashing on every side, it pours out an abundant mass of water equally, and refreshes this earth.

9. And all herbs which have sprung up on the face of the earth, all grasses, shrubs, forest trees, other trees small and great;

10. The various field fruits and whatever is green; all plants on hills, in caves and thickets;

11. All those grasses, shrubs, and trees are vivified by the cloud that both refreshes the thirsty earth and waters the herbs.

12. Grasses and shrubs absorb the water of one essence which issues from the cloud according to their faculty and reach.

13. And all trees, great, small, and mean (middle sized), drink that water according to their growth and faculty, and grow lustily.

14. The great plants whose trunk, stalk, bark, twigs, pith, and leaves are moistened by the water from the cloud develop their blossoms and fruits.

15. They yield their products, each according to its own faculty, reach, and the particular nature of the germ; still the water emitted from the cloud is of but one essence.

16. In the same way, Kasyapa, the Buddha comes into the world like a rain-cloud, and, once born, he, the world's Leader, speaks and shows the real course of life.

17. And the great Seer, honoured in the world, including the gods, speaks thus: 'I am the Tathagata, the highest of men, the Jina. I have appeared in this world like a cloud.

18. 'I shall refresh all beings whose bodies are withered, who are clogged to the triple world. I shall bring to felicity those that are pining away with toils,

give them pleasures and final rest.

19. 'Hear me, O gods and men. Approach to behold me as I am the Tathagata, Bhagavat, who has no superior, who appears in this world to save.

20. 'To thousands of kotis of living beings I preach a pure and most bright law that has but one scope, to wit, deliverance and rest.

21. 'I preach with ever the same voice, constantly taking enlightenment as my text. For this is equal for all; no partiality is in it, neither hatred nor affection.

22. 'I am inexorable, bear no love nor hatred towards any one, and proclaim the law to all creatures without distinction, to the one as well as the other.

23. 'Whether walking, standing, or sitting, I am exclusively occupied with this task of proclaiming the law. I never get tired of sitting on the chair I have ascended.

24. 'I recreate the whole world like a cloud shedding its water without distinction; I have the same feelings for respectable people as for the low; for moral persons as for the immoral;

25. 'For the depraved as for those who observe the rules of good conduct; for those who hold sectarian views and unsound tenets as for those whose views are sound and correct.

26. 'I preach the law to the inferior as well as to persons of superior understanding and extraordinary faculties; inaccessible to weariness, I spread in season the rain of the law.

27. 'After hearing me, each according to his faculty, the several beings find their determined place in various situations, amongst gods, men, beautiful beings, amongst Indras, Brahmas, or the monarchs, rulers of the

universe.'

28. Now I am going to explain what is meant by those plants of different size, some of them being low in the world, others middle-sized and great.

29. Small plants are called the men who walk in the knowledge of the law, which is free from evil after the attaining of Nirvana, who possess the six transcendent faculties and the triple science.

30. Plants of middle size are called the men who, dwelling in mountain caverns, covet the state of a Pratyekabuddha, and whose intelligence is moderately purified.

31. Those who aspire to become leading men thinking: 'I will become a Buddha, a Chief of gods and men, and who practise exertion and meditation,' are called the highest plants.

32. But the sons of Buddha, who sedulously practise benevolence and a peaceful conduct, who have arrived at certainty about their being leading men, these are called trees.

33. Those who move forward the wheel that never rolls back, and with manly strength stand firm in the exercise of miraculous power, releasing many kotis of beings, those are called great trees.

34. Yet it is one and the same law which is preached by the Jina, like the water emitted by the cloud is one and the same; different only are the faculties as described, just as the plants on the face of the earth.

35. By this parable you may understand the skilfulness of the Tathagata, how he preaches one law, the various developments whereof may be likened to drops of rain.

36. I also pour out rain: the rain of the law by which this whole world is refreshed; and each according to his faculty takes to heart this wellspoken law that is one in its essence.

37. Even as all grasses and shrubs, as well as plants of middle size, trees and great trees at the time of rain look bright in all quarters;

38. S"o it is the very nature of the law to promote the everlasting good of the world; by the law the whole world is recreated, and as the plants when refreshed expand their blossoms, the world does the same when refreshed.

39. The plants that in their growth remain middle-sized, are the Arhats stopping when they have overcome frailties, and the Pratyekabuddhas who, living in woody thickets, accomplish this well-spoken law.

40. But many Bodhisattvas who, thoughtful and wise, go their way all over the triple world, striving after supreme enlightenment, they continue increasing in growth like trees.

41. Those who, endowed with magical powers and being adepts in the four degrees of meditation, feel delight at hearing of complete voidness and emit thousands of rays, they are called the great trees on earth.

42. So then, Kasyapa, is the preaching of the law, like the water poured out by the cloud everywhere alike; by which plants and men thrive, endless and eternal blossoms are produced.

43. I reveal the law which has its cause in itself; at due time I show Buddha-enlightenment; this is my supreme skilfulness and that of all leaders of the world.

44. What I here say is true in the highest sense of the word; all my disciples attain Nirvana; by following the sublime path of enlightenment all my

disciples shall become Buddhas.

"And further, Kasyapa, the Tathagata, in his educating creatures, is equal (impartial) and not unequal (partial). As the light of the sun and moon, Kasyapa, shines upon all the world, upon the virtuous and the wicked, upon high and low, upon the fragrant and the ill-smelling; as their beams are sent down upon everything equally, without inequality (partiality); so, too, Kasyapa, the intellectual light of the knowledge of the omniscient, the Tathagatas, the Arhats, the preaching of the true law proceeds equally in respect to all beings in the five states of existence, to all who according to their particular disposition are devoted to the great vehicle, or to the vehicle of the Pratyekabuddhas, or to the vehicle of the disciples. Nor is there any deficiency or excess in the brightness of the Tathagataknowledge up to one's becoming fully acquainted with the law. There are not three vehicles, Kasyapa; there are but beings who act differently; therefore it is declared that there are three vehicles."

When Bhagavat had thus spoken, the venerable Maha-Kasyapa said to him: "O Bhagavat, if there are not three vehicles, for what reason then is the designation of disciples (Sravakas), Buddhas, and Bodhisattvas kept up in the present times?"

On this speech Bhagavat answered the venerable Maha-Kasyapa as follows: "It is, Kasyapa, as if a potter made different vessels out of the same clay. Some of those pots are to contain sugar, others ghee, others curds and milk; others, of inferior quality, are vessels of impurity. There is no diversity in the clay used; no, the diversity of the pots is only due to the substances which are put into each of them. In like manner, Kasyapa, is there but one vehicle, the Buddha-vehicle; there is no second vehicle, no third."

Bhagavat having thus spoken, the venerable Maha-Kasyapa said: "O Bhagavt, if the beings are of different disposition, will there be for those who have left the triple world one Nirvana, or two, or three?"

Bhagavat replied: "Nirvana, Kasyapa, is a consequence of understanding that all phenomena (things) are equal. Hence there is but one Nirvana, not two, not three. Therefore, Kasyapa, I will tell you a parable, for men of good understanding will generally readily enough catch the meaning of what is taught under the shape of a parable.

"It is a case, Kasyapa, similar to that of a certain blind-born man, who says: 'There are no handsome or ugly shapes; there are no men able to see handsome or ugly shapes; there exists no sun nor moon; there are no asterisms nor planets; there are no men able to see planets.' But other persons say to the blind-born: 'There are handsome and ugly shapes; there are men able to see handsome and ugly shapes; there is a sun and moon; there are asterisms and planets; there are men able to see planets.' But the blind-born does not believe them, nor accept what they say. Now there is a physician who knows all diseases. He sees that blind-born man and makes to himself this reflection: 'The disease of this man originates in his sinful actions in former times. All diseases possible to arise are fourfold: rheumatical, cholerical, phlegmatical, and caused by a complication of the corrupted humours.' The physician, after thinking again and again on a means to cure the disease, makes to himself this reflection: 'Surely, with the drugs in common use it is impossible to cure this disease, but there are in the Himalaya, the king of mountains, four herbs, to wit: first, one called Possessed-of-all-sorts-of-colours-and-flavours; second, Delivering-from-all-diseases; third, Delivering-from-all-poisons; fourth, Procuring-happiness-to-those-standing-in-the-right-place.' As the physician feels compassion for the blind-born man he contrives some device to get to the Himalaya, the king of mountains. There he goes up and down and across to search. In doing so he finds the four herbs. One he gives after chewing it with the teeth; another after pounding; another after having it mixed with another drug and boiled; another after having it mixed with a raw drug; another after piercing with a lancet somewhere a vein; another after singeing it in fire; another after combining it with various other substances so as to enter in a compound potion. Owing to these means being applied the blindborn recovers his eyesight, and in consequence of that recovery he sees outwardly and inwardly, far and near, the shine of sun and moon, the asterisms, planets, and all phenomena. Then he says: 'O how foolish was I that I did not believe what they told me, nor accepted what they affirmed. Now I see all; I am delivered from my blindness and have recovered my eyesight; there is none in the world who could surpass me.' And at the same moment Seers of the five transcendent faculties (senses), strong in the divine sight and hearing, in the knowledge of others' minds, in the memory of former abodes, in magical science and intuition, speak to the man thus: 'Good man, you have just recovered thine eyesight, nothing more, and do not know yet anything. Whence comes this conceitedness to you? You have no wisdom, nor you are a clever man.' Further they say to him: 'Good man, when sitting in the interior of your room, you can not see, nor distinguish forms outside, nor discern which beings are animated with kind feelings and which with hostile feelings; you can not distinguish, nor hear at the distance of five yoganas the voice of a man or the sound of a drum, conch trumpet, and the like; you can not even walk as far as a kos without lifting up your feet; you have been produced and developed in your mother's womb without remembering the fact; how then would you be clever, and how can you say that you see all? Good man, you took the darkness for light, and light for darkness.

"Whereupon the Seers are asked by the man: 'By what means and by what good work shall I acquire such wisdom and with your favour acquire those good virtues?' And the Seers say to that man: 'If that is your wish, go and live in the wilderness or take thine abode in mountain caves, to meditate on the law and cast off evil passions. So you will become endowed with the virtues of an ascetic and acquire the transcendent faculties.' The man catches their meaning and becomes an ascetic. Living in the wilderness, the mind intent upon one sole object, he shakes off worldly desires, and acquires the five transcendent faculties. After that acquisition he reflects thus: 'Formerly I did not do the right thing; hence no good accrued to me. Now, however, I can go whither my mind prompts me; formerly I was ignorant, of little understanding, in fact, a blind man.'

"Such, Kasyapa, is the parable I have invented to make you understand my meaning. The moral to be drawn from it is as follows. The word 'blindborn' is a designation for the creatures staying in the whirl of the world with its six states, the creatures who do not know the true law and are heaping up the thick darkness of evil passions. Those are blind from ignorance, and in consequence of it they build up conceptions; in consequence of the latter name-and-form, and so forth, up to the genesis of this whole huge mass of evils.

"So the creatures blind from ignorance remain in the whirl of life, but the Tathagata, who is out of the triple world, feels compassion, prompted by which, like a father for his dear and only son, he appears in the triple world and sees with his eye of wisdom that the creatures are revolving in the circle of the mundane whirl, and are toiling without finding the right means to escape from the rotation. And on seeing this he comes to the conclusion that living beings, according to the good works they have done in former states, have feeble aversions and strong attachments; or feeble attachments and strong aversions; some have little wisdom, others are clever; some have soundly developed views, others have unsound views. To all of them the Tathagata skilfully shows three vehicles.

"The Seers in the parable, those possessing the five transcendent faculties and clear-sight, are the Bodhisattvas who produce enlightened thought, and by the acquirement of acquiescence in the eternal law awake us to supreme, perfect enlightenment.

"The great physician in the parable is the Tathagata. To the blind-born may be likened the creatures blind with infatuation. Attachment, aversion, and infatuation are likened to rheum, bile, and phlegm. The sixty-two false theories also must be looked upon as such. The four herbs are like voidness, causelessness, unfixedness, and reaching Nirvana. Just as by using different drugs different diseases are healed, so by developing the idea of voidness, purposelessness, unfixedness, which are the principles of emancipation, is ignorance suppressed; the suppression of ignorance is succeeded by the suppression of conceptions; and so forth, up to the suppression of the whole huge mass of evils. And thus one's mind will dwell no more on good nor on evil.

"To the man who recovers his eyesight is likened the votary of the vehicle of the disciples and of Pratyekabuddhas. He rends the ties of evil passion in the whirl of the world; freed from those ties he is released from the triple world with its six states of existence. Therefore the votary of the vehicle of the disciples may think and speak thus: There are no more laws to be penetrated; I have reached Nirvana. Then the Tathagata preaches to him: 'How can he who has not penetrated all laws have reached Nirvana?' Bhagavat rouses him to enlightenment, and the disciple, when the consciousness of enlightenment has been awakened in him, no longer stays in the mundane whirl, but at the same time has not yet reached Nirvana. As he has arrived at true insight, he looks upon this triple world in every direction as void, resembling the produce of magic, similar to a dream, a mirage, an echo. He sees that all laws and phenomena are unborn and undestroyed, not bound and not loose, not dark and not bright. He who views the profound laws in such a light, sees, as if he were not seeing, the whole triple world full of beings of contrary and omnifarious fancies and dispositions."

And on that occasion, in order to more amply explain the same subject, Bhagavat uttered the following stanzas:

45. As the rays of the sun and moon descend alike on all men, good and bad, without deficiency in one case or surplus in the other;

46. So the wisdom of the Tathagata shines like the sun and moon, leading all beings without partiality.

47. As the potter, making clay vessels, produces from the same clay pots for sugar, milk, ghee, or water;

48. Some for impurities, others for curdled milk, the clay used by the artificer for the vessels being of but one sort;

49. As a vessel is made to receive all its distinguishing qualities according to the quality of the substance laid into it, so the Tathagatas, on account of the diversity of taste,

50. Mention a diversity of vehicles, though the Buddha-vehicle be the only indisputable one. He who ignores the rotation of mundane existence, has no perception of blessed rest;

51. But he who understands that all laws are void and without reality and without individual character penetrates the enlightenment of the perfectly enlightened Buddhas in its very essence.

52. One who occupies a middle position of wisdom is called a PratyekaJina (Pratyekabuddha); one lacking the insight of voidness is termed a disciple.

53. But after understanding all laws one is called a perfectly-enlightened one; such a one is assiduous in preaching the law to living beings by means of hundreds of devices.

54. It is as if some blind-born man, because he sees no sun, moon, planets, and stars, in his blind ignorance should say: 'There are no visible things at all.'

55. But a great physician taking compassion on the blind man, goes to the Himalaya, where seeking across, up and down,

56. He fetches from the mountain four plants; the herb Of-all-colours-flavours-and-cases, and others. These he intends to apply.

57. He applies them in this manner: one he gives to the blind man after chewing it, another after pounding, again another by introducing it with the point of a needle into the man's body.

58. The man having got his eyesight, sees the sun, moon, planets, and stars, and arrives at the conclusion that it was from sheer ignorance that he spoke thus as he had formerly done.

59. In the same way do people of great ignorance, blind from their birth, move in the turmoil of the world, because they do not know the wheel of causes and effects, the path of toils.

60. In the world so blinded by ignorance appears the highest of those who know all, the Tathagata, the great physician, of compassionate nature.

61. As an able teacher he shows the true law; he reveals supreme Buddha-enlightenment to him who is most advanced.

62. To those of middling wisdom the Leader preaches a middling enlightenment; again another enlightenment he recommends to him who is afraid of the mundane whirl.

63. The disciple who by his discrimination has escaped from the triple world thinks he has reached pure Nirvana, but it is only by knowing all laws that the immortal Nirvana is reached.

64. In that case it is as if the great Seers, moved by compassion, said to him: 'You are mistaken; do not be proud of your knowledge.

65. 'When you are in the interior of your room, you can not perceive what is going on without, fool as you are.

66. 'You who, when staying within, do not perceive even now what people outside are doing or not doing, how would you be wise, fool as you are?

67. 'You are not able to hear a sound at a distance of but five yoganas, far less at a greater distance.

68. 'You can not discern who are malevolent or benevolent towards you. Whence then comes that pride to you?

69. 'If you have to walk so far as a kos, you can not go without a beaten track; and what happened to you when in your mother's womb you have immediately forgotten.

70. 'In this world he is called all-knowing who possesses the five transcendent faculties, but when you who know nothing pretendest to be all knowing, it is an effect of infatuation.

71. 'If you are desirous of omniscience, direct your attention to transcendent wisdom; then betake yourself to the wilderness and meditate on the pure law; by it you shall acquire the transcendent faculties.'

72. The man catches the meaning, goes to the wilderness, meditates with the greatest attention, and, as he is endowed with good qualities, acquires the five transcendent faculties.

73. Similarly all disciples fancy having reached Nirvana, but the Jina instructs them by saying: 'This is a temporary repose, not a final rest.'

74. It is an artifice of the Buddhas to enunciate this dogma. There is no real Nirvana without all-knowingness; try to reach this.

75. The boundless knowledge of the three paths of time, the six utmost perfections Paramitas, voidness, the absence of purpose or object, the

absence of finiteness;

76. The idea of enlightenment and the other laws leading to Nirvana, both such as are mixed with imperfection and such as are exempt from it, such as are tranquil and comparable to ethereal space;

77. The four Brahmaviharas and the four Sangrahas, as well as the laws sanctioned by eminent sages for the education of creatures;

78. He who knows these things and that all phenomena have the nature of illusion and dreams, that they are pithless as the stem of the plantain and similar to an echo;

79. And who knows that the triple world throughout is of that nature, he knows rest.

80. He who considers all laws to be alike, void, devoid of particularity and individuality, not derived from an intelligent cause; nay, who discerns that nothingness is law;

81. Such a one has great wisdom and sees the whole of the law entirely. There are no three vehicles by any means; there is but one vehicle in this world.

82. All laws are alike, equal, for all, and ever alike. Knowing this, one understands immortal Nirvana.

PART VI.

ANNOUNCEMENT OF FUTURE DESTINY

After pronouncing these stanzas Bhagavat addressed the complete assembly of monks: "I announce to you, O monks, I make known to you that the monk Kasyapa, my disciple, here present, shall do homage to thirty thousand kotis of Buddhas; he shall respect, honour, and worship them; and he shall keep the true law of those Buddhas. In his last bodily existence in the world Avabhasa (Lustrous), in the age of Mahavyuha (Great Division) he shall be a Tathagata, an Arhat, by the name of Rasmiprabhasa (One Beaming With Rays). His lifetime shall last twelve intermediate kalpas, and his true law twenty intermediate kalpas; the counterfeit of his true law shall last as many intermediate kalpas. His Buddha-fields will be pure, clean, devoid of stones, grit, gravel, devoid of pits and precipices, devoid of gutters and dirty pools; even, pretty, beautiful, and pleasant to see; consisting of lapis lazuli, adorned with jewel-trees, and looking like a checker-board with eight compartments set off with gold threads. It will be strewed with flowers, and many hundred thousand Bodhisattvas are to appear in it. As to disciples, there will be innumerable hundred thousands of myriads of kotis of them. Neither Mara the Evil One, nor his host will be discoverable in it, though Mara and his followers shall afterwards be there; for they will apply themselves to receive the true law under the command of that very Lord Rasmiprabhasa."

And on that occasion Bhagavat uttered the following stanzas:

1. With my Buddha-eye, monks, I see that Kasyapa here shall become a Buddha at a future epoch, in an incalculable Eon, after he shall have paid homage to the most high of men.

2. This Kasyapa shall see fully thirty thousand kotis of Jinas, under whom he shall lead a spiritual life for the sake of Buddha-knowledge.

3. After having paid homage to those highest of men and acquired that

104

supreme knowledge, he shall in his last bodily existence be a Leader of the world, a matchless, great Seer.

4. And his field will be magnificent, excellent, pure, goodly, beautiful, pretty, nice, ever delightful, and set off with gold threads.

5. That field, O monks, appearing like a board divided into eight compartments, will have several jewel-trees, one in each compartment, from which issues a delicious odour.

6. It will be adorned with plenty of flowers, and embellished with variegated blossoms; in it are no pits nor precipices; it is even, goodly, beautiful.

7. There will be found hundreds of kotis of Bodhisattvas, subdued of mind and of great; magical power, mighty keepers of Sutra of great extension.

8. As to disciples, faultless, princes of the law, standing in their last period of life, their number can never be known, even if one should go on counting for Eons, and that with the aid of divine knowledge.

9. He himself shall stay twelve intermediate kalpas, and his true law twenty complete Eons; the counterfeit is to continue as many Eons in the domain of Rasmiprabhasa.

Thereupon the venerable Maha-Maudgalyayana, the venerable Subhuti, and the venerable Maha-Katyayana, with their bodies trembling, gazed up to Bhagavat and at the same moment severally uttered, in mental concert, the following stanzas :

10. O Arhat, great Hero, Sakya-lion, the highest of men! Out of compassion to us speak the Buddha-word.

11. The highest of men, the Jina, he who knows the fatal term, will, as

it were, sprinkle us with nectar by predicting our destiny also.

12. It is as if a certain man, in time of famine, comes and gets good food, but to whom, when the food is already in his hands, they say that he should wait.

13. Similarly it was with us, who after minding the lower vehicle, at the calamitous conjuncture of a bad time, were longing for Buddha-knowledge.

14. But the perfectly-enlightened great Seer has not yet favoured us with a prediction of our destiny, as if he would say: 'Do not eat the food that has been put into your hand.'

15. Quite so, O great Hero, we were longing as we heard the exalted voice and thought: 'Then shall we be at rest and felicitous, blessed, beatified, when we shall have received a prediction.'

16. Utter a prediction, O great Hero, so benevolent and merciful! Let there be an end of our feeling of poverty!"

And Bhagavat, who in his mind apprehended the thoughts arising in the minds of those great senior disciples, again addressed the complete assembly of monks: "This great disciple of mine, O monks, the senior Subhuti, shall likewise pay homage to thirty hundred thousand myriads of kotis of Buddhas; shall show them respect, honour, reverence, veneration, and worship. Under them shall he lead a spiritual life and achieve enlightenment. After the performance of such duties shall he, in his last bodily existence, become a Tathagata in the world, an Arhat, by the name of Sasiketu (Moon-signal).

"His Buddha-fields will be called Ratnasambhava and his epoch Ratnaprabhasa. And that Buddha-fields will be even, beautiful, crystalline, variegated with jewel-trees, devoid of pits and precipices, devoid of sewers, nice, covered with flowers. And there will men have their abode in palaces given them for their use. In it will be many disciples, innumerable, so that it would be impossible to terminate the calculation. Many hundred thousand myriads of kotis of Bodhisattvas also will be there. The lifetime of that Lord is to last twelve intermediate kalpas; his true law is to continue twenty intermediate kalpas and its counterfeit as many. That Leader will, while standing poised in the firmament, preach the law to the monks and educate many thousands of Bodhisattvas and disciples."

And on that occasion Bhagavat uttered the following stanzas:

17. I have something to announce, O monks, something to make known; listen then to me. The senior Subhuti, my disciple, shall in days to come be a Buddha.

18. After having seen of most mighty Buddhas thirty myriads of kotis in full, he shall enter upon the straight course to obtain this knowledge.

19. In his last bodily existence shall the hero, possessed of the thirty-two distinctive signs, become a great Seer, similar to a column of gold, beneficial and bounteous to the world.

20. The field where that friend of the world shall save myriads of kotis of living beings will be most beautiful, pretty, and delightful to people at large.

21. In it will be many Bodhisattvas to turn the wheel that never rolls back; endowed with keen faculties they will, under that Jina, be the ornaments of the Buddha-fields.

22. His disciples are so numerous as to pass calculation and measure, gifted with the six transcendent faculties, the triple science and magic power, firm in the eight emancipations.

23. His magic power, while he reveals supreme enlightenment, is inconceivable. Gods and men, as numerous as the sands of the Ganges, will

always reverentially salute him with joined hands.

24. He shall stay twelve intermediate kalpas; the true law of that most high of men is to last twenty intermediate kalpas and the counterfeit of it as many."

Again Bhagavat addressed the complete assembly of monks: "I announce to you, O monks, I make known that the senior Maha-Katyayana here present, my disciple, shall pay homage to eight thousand kotis of Buddhas; shall show them respect, honour, reverence, veneration, and worship; at the expiration of those Tathagatas he shall build Stupas, a thousand yoganas in height, fifty yoganas in circumference, and consisting of seven precious substances: gold, silver, lapis lazuli, crystal, red pearl, emerald, and coral. Those Stupas he shall worship with flowers, incense, perfumed wreaths, ointments, powder, robes, umbrellas, banners, flags, triumphal streamers. Afterwards he shall again pay a similar homage to twenty kotis of Buddhas, show them respect, honour, reverence, veneration, and worship. Then in his last bodily existence, his last corporeal appearance, he shall be a Tathagata in the world, an Arhat, named Gambunada-prabhasa (Gold-shined), endowed with science and conduct. His Buddha-fields will be thoroughly pure, even, nice, pretty, beautiful, crystalline, variegated with jeweltrees, interlaced with gold threads, strewed with flowers, free from beings of the brute creation, hell, and the host of demons, replete with numerous men and gods, adorned with many hundred thousand disciples and many hundred thousand Bodhisattvas. The measure of his lifetime shall be twelve intermediate kalpas; his true law shall continue twenty intermediate kalpas and its counterfeit as many."

And on that occasion Bhagavat uttered the following stanzas:

25. Listen all to me, O monks, since I am going to utter an infallible word . Katyayana here, the senior, my disciple, shall render worship to the Leaders.

26. He shall show veneration of various kinds and in many ways to the

Leaders, after whose expiration he shall build Stupas, worshipping them with flowers and perfumes.

27. In his last bodily existence he shall be a Jina, in a thoroughly pure field, and after acquiring full knowledge he shall preach to a thousand kotis of living beings.

28. He shall be a mighty Buddha and illuminator, highly honoured in this world, including the gods, under the name of Gambunada-prabhasa, and save kotis of gods and men.

29. Many Bodhisattvas as well as disciples, beyond measure and calculation, will in that field adorn the reign of that Buddha, all of them freed from existence and exempt from existence."

Again Bhagavat addressed the complete assembly of monks: "I announce to you, O monks, I make known, that the senior Maha-Maudgalyayana here present, my disciple, shall propitiate twenty-eight thousand Buddhas and pay those Leaders homage of various kinds; he shall show them respect, and after their expiration build Stupas consisting of seven precious substances: gold, silver, lapis lazuli, crystal, red pearl, emerald, and coral; Stupas a thousand yoganas in height and five hundred yoganas in circumference, which Stupas he shall worship in different ways, with flowers, incense, perfumed wreaths, ointments, powder, robes, umbrellas, banners, flags, and triumphal streamers.

"Afterwards he shall again pay a similar worship to twenty hundred thousand kotis of Buddhas; he shall show respect, and in his last bodily existence become in the world a Tathagata, named Tamalapatrakandanagandha, endowed with science and conduct.. The field of that Buddha will be called Manobhirama; his period Ratipratipurna. And that Buddha-fields will be even, nice, pretty, beautiful, crystalline, variegated with jewel-trees, strewn with detached flowers, replete with gods and men, frequented by hundred thousands of Seers, that is to say, disciples and Bodhisattvas. The measure of his lifetime shall be twenty-four intermediate kalpas; his true law is to last forty intermediate kalpas and its counterfeit as many."

And on that occasion Bhagavat uttered the following stanzas:

30. The scion of the Mudgala-race, my disciple here, after leaving human existence shall see twenty thousand mighty Jinas and eight thousand more of these faultless beings.

31. Under them he shall follow a course of duty, trying to reach Buddha-knowledge; he shall pay homage in various ways to those Leaders and to the most high of men.

32. After keeping their true law, of wide reach and sublime, for thousands of kotis of Eons, he shall at the expiration of those, Buddhas worship their Stupas.

33. In honour of those most high Jinas, those mighty beings I so beneficial to the world, he shall erect Stupas consisting of precious substances, and decorated with triumphal streamers, worshipping them with flowers, perfumes, and the sounds of music.

34. At the period of his last bodily existence he shall, in a nice and beautiful field, be a Buddha bounteous and compassionate to the world, under the name of Tamalapatrakandanagandha.

35. The measure of that Buddha's life shall be fully twenty-four intermediate kalpas, during which he shall be assiduous in declaring the Buddha-rule to men and gods.

36. That Jina shall have many thousands of kotis of disciples, innumerable as the sands of the Ganges, gifted with the six transcendent faculties and the

triple science, and possessed of magic power, under the command of that Buddha.

37. Under the reign of that Buddha there shall also appear numerous Bodhisattvas, many thousands of them, unable to slide back, developing zeal, of extensive knowledge and studious habits.

38. After that Jina's expiration his true law shall measure in time twenty-four intermediate kalpas in full; its counterfeit shall have the same measure.

39. These are my five mighty disciples whom I have destined to supreme enlightenment and to become in future self-born Jinas; now hear from me their course. (In this chapter only four disciples are mentioned; the fifth must be Sariputra, whose destination has been predicted before).

PART VII.

ANCIENT DEVOTION

"You, O monks, in the past, incalculable, more than incalculable, inconceivable, immense, measureless Eons since, nay, at a period, an epoch far beyond, there appeared in the world a Tathagata, named Mahabhignagnanabhibhu, endowed with science and conduct, a Buddha, in the sphere Sambhava (Origin, genesis), in the period Maharupa. You ask, O monks, how long ago is it that the Tathagata was born? Well, suppose some man was to reduce to powder the whole mass of the earth element as much as is to be found in this whole universe; that after taking one atom of dust from this world he is to walk a thousand worlds farther in easterly direction to deposit that single atom; that after taking a second atom of dust and walking a thousand worlds farther he deposits that second atom, and proceeding in this way at last gets the whole of the earth element deposited in eastern direction. Now, O monks, what do you think of it, is it possible by calculation to find the end or limit of these worlds?"

They answered: 'Certainly not, Bhagavat; certainly not, Buddha."

Bhagavat said: "On the contrary, O monks, some arithmetician or master of arithmetic might, indeed, be able by calculation to find the end or limit of the worlds, both those where the atoms have been deposited and where they have not, but it is impossible by applying the rules of arithmetic to find the limit of those hundred thousands of myriads of Eons, so long, so inconceivable, so immense is the number of Eons which have elapsed since the expiration of that Lord, the Tathagata Mahabhignagnanabhibhu. Yet, O monks, I perfectly remember that Tathagata who has been extinct for so long a time, as if he had reached extinction today or yesterday, because of my possessing the mighty knowledge and sight of the Tathagata."

And on that occasion Bhagavat pronounced the following stanzas:

1. I remember the great Seer Abhignagnanabhibhu, the most high of men, who existed many kotis of Eons ago as the superior Jina of the period.

2. If, for example, some men after reducing this universe to atoms of dust took one atom to deposit it a thousand regions farther on;

3. If he deposited a second, a third atom, and so proceeded until he had done with the whole mass of dust, so that this world were empty and the mass of dust exhausted;

4. To that immense mass of the dust of these worlds, entirely reduced to atoms, I liken the number of Eons past.

5. So immense is the number of kotis of Eons past since that extinct Buddha; the whole of existing atoms is no adequate expression of it; so many are the Eons which have expired since.

6. That Leader who has expired so long ago, those disciples and Bodhisattvas, I remember all of them as if it were today or yesterday. Such is the knowledge of the Tathagatas.

7. So endless, monks, is the knowledge of the Tathagata; I know what has taken place many hundreds of Eons ago, by my precise and faultless memory.

"To proceed, O monks, the measure of the lifetime of the Tathagata Mahabhignagnanabhibhu, the Arhat, was fifty-four hundred thousand myriads of kotis of Eons.

"In the beginning when Bhagavat had not yet reached supreme, perfect enlightenment and had just occupied the summit of the terrace of enlightenment, he discomfited and defeated the whole host of Mara, after which he thought: 'I am to reach perfect enlightenment.' But those laws of perfect enlightenment had not yet dawned upon him. He stayed on the terrace of enlightenment at the foot of the tree of enlightenment during one intermediate kalpa. He stayed there a second, a third intermediate kalpa, but did not yet attain supreme, perfect enlightenment. He remained a fourth, a fifth, a sixth, a seventh, an eighth, a ninth, a tenth intermediate kalpa on the terrace of enlightenment at the foot of the tree of enlightenment, continuing sitting cross-legged without in the meanwhile rising. He stayed, the mind motionless, the body unstirring and untrembling, but those laws had not yet dawned upon him.

"Now, O monks, while Bhagavat was just on the summit of the terrace of enlightenment, the gods of Paradise (Trayastrimsas) prepared him a magnificent royal throne, a hundred yoganas high, on occupying which Bhagavat attained supreme, perfect enlightenment; and no sooner had Bhagavat occupied the seat of enlightenment than the Brahmakayika gods scattered a rain of flowers all around the seat of enlightenment over a distance of a hundred yoganas; in the sky they let loose storms by which the flowers, withered, were swept away. From the beginning of the rain of flowers, while Bhagavat was sitting on the seat of enlightenment, it poured without interruption during fully ten intermediate kalpas, covering Bhagavat. That rain of flowers having once begun falling continued to the moment of Bhagavat's complete Nirvana. The angels belonging to the division of the four guardians of the cardinal points made the celestial drums of the gods resound; they made them resound without interruption in honour of Bhagavat who had attained the summit of the terrace of enlightenment. Thereafter, during fully ten intermediate kalpas, they made uninterruptedly resound those celestial musical instruments up to the moment of the complete extinction of Bhagavat.

"Again, monks, after the lapse of ten intermediate kalpas Bhagavat Mahabhignagnanabhibhu, the Tathagata, reached supreme, perfect enlightenment. Immediately on knowing his having become enlightened the sixteen sons born to that Lord when a prince royal, the eldest of whom was named Gnanakara-which sixteen young princes, monks, had severally toys to play with, variegated and pretty-those sixteen princes, I repeat, monks, left their toys, their amusements, and since they knew that Bhagavat Mahabhignagnanabhibhu, the Tathagata, had attained supreme, perfect knowledge, went, surrounded and attended by their weeping mothers and nurses, along with the noble, rich king Kakravartin, many ministers, and hundred thousands of myriads of kotis of living beings, to the place where Bhagavat Mahabhignagnanabhibhu, the Tathagata, was seated on the summit of the terrace of enlightenment. They went up to Bhagavat in order to honour, respect, worship, revere, and venerate him, saluted his feet with their heads, made three turns round him keeping him to the right, lifted up their joined hands, and praised Bhagavat, face to face, with the following stanzas:

8. You are the great physician, having no superior, rendered perfect in endless Eons. your benign wish of saving all mortals from darkness has today been fulfilled.

9. Most difficult things hast you achieved during the ten intermediate kalpas now past; you have been sitting all that time without once moving your body, hand, foot, or any other part.

10.Your mind also was tranquil and steady, motionless, never to be shaken; you knew no distraction; you are completely quiet and faultless.

11. Joy with you! That you so happily and safely, without any hurt, have reached supreme enlightenment. How great a fortune is ours! We congratulate ourselves, O Lion amongst kings!

12. These unhappy creatures, vexed in all ways, deprived of eyes, as it were, and joyless, do not find the road leading to the end of toils, nor develop energy for the sake of deliverance.

13. Dangers are for a long time on the increase and the phenomena (things) are deprived of the possession of a celestial body; the word of the Jina is not being heard; the whole world is plunged in thick darkness.

14. But now you, Majesty of the world, have reached this hallowed, high, and faultless spot. We as well as the world are obliged to you, and approach to seek our refuge with you, O Protector!'

"When, O monks, those sixteen princes in the condition of boys, childlike and young, had with such stanzas celebrated Bhagavat Mahabhignagnanabhibhu, the Tathagata, they urged Bhagavat to move on the wheel of the law: 'Preach the law, O Bhagavat; preach the law, O Buddha, for the good of the public, the happiness of the public, out of compassion for the world; for the benefit, good, and happiness of the people, both of gods and men.' And on that occasion they uttered the following stanzas:

15. Preach the law, O you who are marked with a hundred auspicious

signs, O Leader, O incomparable great Seer! You have attained exalted, sublime knowledge; let it shine in the world, including the gods.

16. Release us as well as these creatures; display the knowledge of the Tathagatas, that we also and, further, these beings may obtain this supreme enlightenment.

17. You know every course of duty and knowledge; you know the mental and moral disposition and the good works done in a former state; the natural bent of all living beings. Move on the most exalted, sublime wheel!

"Then, monks, as Bhagavat Mahabhignagnanabhibhu, the Tathagata, reached supreme, perfect enlightenment, fifty hundred thousand myriads of kotis of spheres in each of the ten directions of space were shaken in six different ways and became illumined with a great lustre. And in the intervals between all those spheres, in the dreary places of dark gloom, where even the sun and moon, so powerful, mighty, and splendid, have no advantage of the shining power they are endowed with, have no advantage of the colour and brightness they possess, even in those places a great lustre arose instantly. And the beings who appeared in those intervals behold each other, acknowledge each other, and exclaim: 'There are other beings also here appearing! There are other beings also here appearing!' The palaces and aerial cars of the gods in all those spheres up to the Brahma-world shook in six different ways and became illumined with a great lustre, surpassing the divine majesty of the gods. So then, monks, a great earthquake and a great, sublime lustre arose simultaneously. And the aerial cars of the Brahma-angels to the east, in these fifty hundred thousand myriads of kotis of spheres, began excessively to glitter, glow, and sparkle in splendo,ur and glory. And those Brahma-angels made this reflection: 'What may be foreboded by these aerial cars so excessively glittering, glowing, and sparkling in splendour and glory?' Thereupon, monks, the Brahma-angels in the fifty hundred thousand myriads of kotis of spheres went all to each other's abodes and communicated the matter to one another. After that, monks, the great

Brahma-angel, named Sarvasattvatratri (Saviour of all beings), addressed the numerous host of Brahma-angels in the following stanzas:

18. Our aerial cars now are all bristling with rays in an extraordinary degree, and blazing in beautiful splendour and brilliancy. What may be the cause of it?

19. Come, let us investigate the matter, what divine being has today sprung into existence, whose power, such as was never seen before, here now appears?

20. Or should it be the Buddha, the king of kings, who today has been born somewhere in the world, and whose birth is announced by such a token that all the points of the horizon are now blazing in splendour?'

"Thereupon, monks, the great Brahma-angels in the fifty hundred thousand myriads of kotis of spheres mounted all together their own divine aerial cars, took with them divine bags, as large as Mount Sumeru, with celestial flowers, and went through the four quarters successively until they arrived at the western quarter, where those great Brahma-angels, O monks, stationed in the western quarter, saw Bhagavat Mahabhignagnanabhibhu, the Tathagata, on the summit of the exalted terrace of enlightenment, seated on the royal throne at the foot of the tree of enlightenment, surrounded and attended by gods, Nagas, goblins, Gandharvas, demons, Garudas, Kinnaras, great serpents, men, and beings not human, while his sons, the sixteen young princes, were urging him to move forward the wheel of the law. On seeing which the Brahma-angels came up to Bhagavat, saluted his feet with their heads, walked many hundred thousand times round him from left to right, strewing flowers and overwhelming both him and the tree of enlightenment, over a distance of ten yoganas, with those flower-bags as large as Mount Sumeru. After that they presented to Bhagavat their aerial cars with the words: 'Accept, O Bhagavat, these aerial cars out of compassion to us. Use, O Buddha, those cars out of compassion to us.'

"On that occasion, O monks, after presenting their own cars to Bhagavat, the Brahma-angels celebrated Bhagavat, face to face, with the following seasonable stanzas:

21. The wonderful, matchless Jina, so beneficial and merciful, has arisen in the world. You are born a protector, a ruler, a teacher, a master. Today all quarters are blessed.

22. We have come as far as fully fifty thousand kotis of worlds from here to humbly salute the Jina by surrendering our lofty aeriel cars all together.

23. We possess these variegated and bright cars, owing to previous works; accept them to oblige us, and make use of them to your heart's content, O Knower of the world!'

"After the great Brahma-angels, monks, had celebrated Bhagavat Mahabhignagnanabhibhu, the Tathagata, face to face, with these seasonable stanzas, they besought him, saying: 'May Bhagavat move forward the wheel of the law! May Bhagavat preach final rest! May Bhagavat release all beings! Be favourable, O Bhagavat, to this world! Preach the law, O Bhagavat, to this world, including gods, Maras, and Brahma-angels; to all people, including ascetics and Brahmans, gods, men, and demons! It will tend to the good of the public, to the happiness of the public; out of mercy to the world, for the benefit and happiness of the people at large, both gods and men.'

"Thereupon, monks, those fifty hundred thousand myriads of kotis of Brahma-angels addressed Bhagavat, with one voice, in common chorus, with the following stanza:

24. Show the law, O Bhagavat. Show it, O the highest of men! Show the power of your kindness. Save the tormented beings!

25. Rare is the light of the world like the blossom of the glomerated fig-tree. You have arisen, O great Hero. We pray to you, the Tathagata.'

"And Bhagavat, O monks, silently intimated his assent to the Brahma-angels.

"Somewhat later, O monks, the aerial cars of the Brahma-angels in the south-eastern quarter in the fifty hundred thousand myriads of spheres began excessively to glitter, glow, and sparkle in splendour and glory. And those Brahma-angels made this reflection: 'What may be foreboded by these aerial cars so excessively glittering, glowing, and sparkling in splendour and glory? Thereupon, monks, the Brahma-angels in the fifty hundred thousand myriads of kotis of spheres went all to each other's abodes and communicated the matter to one another. After that, monks, the great Brahma-angel, named Adhimatrakarunika (Exceedingly compassionate), addressed the numerous host of Brahma-angels with the following stanzas:

26. What foretoken is it we see now friends? Who or what is foreboded by the celestial cars shining with such uncommon glory?

27. May, perhaps, some blessed divine being have come hither, by whose power all these aerial cars are illumined?

28. Or may the Buddha, the most high of men, have appeared in this world, that by his power these celestial cars are in such a condition as we see them?

29. Let us all together go and search; no trifle can be the cause of it, as such a foretoken, indeed, was never seen before.

30. Come, let us go and visit kotis of fields, along the four quarters. A Buddha will certainly now have made his appearance in this world.'

"Thereupon, O monks, the great Brahma-angels in the fifty hundred thousand myriads of kotis of spheres mounted all together their own divine aerial cars, took with them divine bags, as large as Mount Sumeru, with celestial flowers, and went through the four quarters successively until they arrived at the north-western quarter, where those great Brahma-angels, stationed in the north-western quarter, saw Bhagavat Mahabhignagnanabhibhu.

"On that occasion, O monks, after presenting their own cars to Bhagavat the Brahma-angels celebrated Bhagavat, face to face, with the following seasonable stanzas:

31. Homage to you, matchless great Seer, whose voice is sweet as the lark's. Leader in the world, including the gods, I salute you, who are so benign and bounteous to the world.

32. How wonderful, O Bhagavat, is it that after so long a time youappearest in the world. Eighty hundred complete Eons this world of the living was without Buddha.

33. It was deprived of the most high of men. Hell was prevailing and the celestial bodies constantly went on waning during eighty hundred complete Eons.

34. But now he has appeared, owing to our good works, who is our eye, refuge, resting-place, protection, father, and kinsman; he, the benign and bounteous one, the King of the law.

"After the great Brahma-angels, monks, had celebrated Bhagavat Mahabhignagnanabhibhu, the Tathagata, face to face, with these seasonable stanzas they besought him: 'May Bhagavat move forward the wheel of the law!'

"Thereupon, monks, those fifty hundred thousand myriads of kotis of Brahma-angels addressed Bhagavat, with one voice, in common chorus, with the following stanzas:

35. Move forward the exalted wheel, O great ascetic! Reveal the law in all directions; deliver all beings oppressed with suffering; produce amongst mortals gladness and joy!

36. Let them by hearing the law partake of enlightenment and reach divine places. Let all shake off their demon body and be peaceful, meek, and at ease.

"And Bhagavat, O monks, silently intimated his assent to these Brahma-angels also.

"Somewhat later, O monks, the aerial cars of the Brahma-angels in the southern quarter have become excessively brilliant. After that, monks, the great Brahma-angel, named Sudharma, addressed the numerous host of Brahma-angels in stanzas:

37. It cannot be without cause or reason, friends, that now all these celestial cars are so brilliant; this bespeaks some portent somewhere in the world. Come, let us go and investigate the matter.

38. No such portent has appeared in hundreds of Eons past. Either some god has been born or a Buddha has arisen in this world.

"Thereupon, O monks, the great Brahma-angels in the fifty hundred thousand myriads of kotis of spheres mounted.

"On that occasion, monks, after presenting their own cars to Bhagavat, the Brahma-angels celebrated Bhagavat, face to face, with the following seasonable stanzas:

39. Most rare and precious is the sight of the Leaders. Be welcome, O dispeller of worldly defilement. It is after a long time that younow appearest in the world; after hundreds of complete Eons one now beholds you.

40. Refresh the thirsty creatures, O Bhagavat of the world! Now first you are seen; it is not easy to behold you. As rare or precious as the flowers of the glomerated fig-tree is your appearance, O Bhagavat.

41. By your power these aerial cars of ours are so uncommonly illumined now, O Leader. To show us your favour accept them, O you whose look pierces everywhere!'

"After the great Brahma-angels, O monks, had celebrated Bhagavat Mahabhignagnanabhibhu, the Tathagata, face to face, with these seasonable stanzas, they besought him: 'May Bhagavat move forward the wheel of the law!'

"Thereupon, monks, those fifty hundred thousand myriads of kotis of Brahma-angels addressed Bhagavat, with one voice, in common chorus, with the following stanzas:

42. Preach the law, O Bhagavat! Move forward the wheel of the law, make the drum of the law resound, and blow the conch-trumpet of the law.

43. Shed the rain of the true law over this world and proclaim the sweet-sounding, good word; manifest the law required, save myriads of kotis of beings.

"And Bhagavat, O monks, silently intimated his assent to the Brahma-angels.

"The same occurred in the south-west, in the west, in the north-west, in the north, in the north-east, in the nadir.

"Then, O monks, the aerial cars of the Brahma-angels in the nadir, in those fifty hundred thousand myriads of kotis of spheres have become excessively brilliant. After that, the great Brahma-angel, named Sikhin, addressed the numerous host of Brahma-angels with the following stanzas:

44. What may be the cause that our cars are so bright with splendour, colour, and light? What may be the reason of their being so exceedingly glorious?

45. We have seen nothing like this before nor heard of it from others. These cars are now bright with splendour and exceedingly glorious; what may be the cause of it?

46. Should it be some god who has been bestowed upon the world in recompense of good works, and whose grandeur thus comes to light? Or is perhaps a Buddha born in the world?

"Thereupon, monks, the great Brahma-angels in the fifty hundred thousand myriads of kotis of spheres mounted all together their own divine aerial cars, took with them divine bags, as large as Mount Sumeru, with celestial flowers, and went through the four quarters successively until they arrived at the zenith, where those great Brahma-angels, stationed at the zenith, saw Bhagavat Mahabhignagnanabhibhu.

"On that occasion, monks, after presenting their own cars to Bhagavat, the Brahma-angels celebrated Bhagavat, face to face, with the following seasonable stanzas:

47. How goodly is the sight of the Buddhas, the mighty Leaders of the world; those Buddhas who are to deliver all beings in this triple world.

48. The all-seeing Masters of the world send their looks in all directions of the horizon, and by opening the gate of immortality they make people reach the safe shore.

49. An inconceivable number of Eons now past were void, and all quarters wrapt in darkness, as the chief Jinas did not appear.

50. The dreary hells, the brute creation and demons were on the increase; thousands of kotis of living beings fell into the state of ghosts.

51. The heavenly bodies were on the wane; after their disappearance they entered upon evil ways; their course became wrong because they did not hear the law of the Buddhas.

52. All creatures lacked dutiful behaviour, purity, good state, and understanding; their happiness was lost, and the consciousness of happiness was gone.

53. They did not observe the rules of morality, were firmly rooted in the false law, not being led by Bhagavat of the world, they were precipitated into a false course.

54. Hail! You have come at last, O Light of the world! You, born to be bounteous towards all beings.

55. Hail! You have safely arrived at supreme Buddha-knowledge; we feel thankful before you, and so does the world, including the gods.

56. By your power, O mighty Chief, our aerial cars are glittering; to you we present them, deign to accept them, O Buddha.

57. Out of grace to us, O Leader, make use of them, so that we, as well as all

other beings, may attain supreme enlightenment.

"After the great Brahma-angels, O monks, had celebrated Bhagavat Mahabhignagnanabhibhu, the Tathagata, face to face, with seasonable stanzas, they besought him: 'May Bhagavat move forward the wheel of the law!'

"Thereupon, monks, those fifty hundred thousand myriads of kotis of Brahma-angels addressed Bhagavat, with one voice, in common chorus, with the following two stanzas:

58. Move forward the exalted, unsurpassed wheel! beat the drum of immortality! Release all beings from hundreds of evils, and show the path of Nirvana.

59. Expound the law we pray for; show your favour to us and this world. Let us hear your sweet and lovely voice which you have exercised during thousands of kotis of Eons.'

"Now, monks, Bhagavat Mahabhignagnanabhibhu the Tathagata, being acquainted with the prayer of the hundred thousand myriads of kotis of Brahma-angels and of the sixteen princes, his sons, commenced at that juncture to turn the wheel that has three turns and twelve parts, the wheel never moved by any ascetic, Brahman, god, demon, nor by any one else. His preaching consisted in this: 'This is pain; this is the origin of pain; this is the suppression of pain; this is the treatment leading to suppression of pain.' He extensively set forth how the series of causes and effects is evolved and said: 'It is thus, monks. From ignorance proceed conceptions; from conceptions proceeds understanding; from understanding name and form; from name and form the six senses; from the six senses proceeds contact; from contact sensation; from sensation proceeds longing; from longing proceeds striving; from striving as cause issues existence; from existence birth; from birth old age, death, mourning, lamentation, sorrow, dismay, and despondency. So originates this whole mass of misery. From the suppression of ignorance results the suppression of conceptions; from the suppression of conceptions results that of understanding; from the suppression of understanding results that of name and form; from the suppression of name and form results that of the six senses; from the suppression of the six senses results that of contact; from the suppression of contact results that of sensation; from the suppression of sensation results that of longing; from the suppression of longing results that of striving; from the suppression of striving results that of existence; from the suppression of existence results that of birth; from the suppression of birth results that of old age, death, mourning, lamentation, sorrow, dismay, and despondency. In this manner the whole mass of misery is suppressed.

"And while this wheel of the law, monks, was being moved onward by Bhagavat Mahabhignagnanabhibhu, the Tathagata, in presence of the world, including the gods, demons, and Brahma-angels, of the assemblage, including ascetics and Brahmans. Then, at that time, on that occasion, the minds of sixty hundred thousand myriads of kotis of living beings were without effort freed from imperfections and became all possessed of the triple science, of the sixfold transcendent wisdom, of the emancipations and meditations. In due course, monks, Bhagavat Mahabhignagnanabhibhu, the Tathagata, again gave a second exposition of the law, likewise a third and a fourth exposition. And at each exposition, monks, the minds of hundred thousands of myriads of kotis of beings, like the sands of the river Ganges, were without effort freed from imperfections. Afterwards, monks, the congregation of disciples of that Lord was so numerous as to surpass all calculation.

"Meanwhile, monks, the sixteen princes, the youths, had full of faith left home to lead the vagrant life of mendicants, and had all of them become novices, clever, bright, intelligent, pious, followers of the course of duty under many hundred thousand Buddhas, and striving after supreme, perfect enlightenment. These sixteen novices, monks, said to Bhagavat Mahabhignagnanabhibhu, the Tathagata, the following: 'O Bhagavat, these many hundred thousand myriads of kotis of disciples of the Tathagata have become very mighty, very powerful, very potent, owing to Bhagavat's teaching of the law. Deign, O Bhagavat, to teach us also, for mercy's sake, the law with a view to supreme, perfect enlightenment, so that we also may follow the teaching of the Tathagata. We want, O Bhagavat, to see the knowledge of the Tathagata; Bhagavat can himself testify to this, for you, O Bhagavat, who knows the disposition of all beings, also knows ours.'

"Then, O monks, on seeing that those princes, the youths, had chosen the vagrant life of mendicants and become novices, the half of the whole retinue of the king Kakravartin, to the number of eighty hundred thousand myriads of kotis of living beings, chose the vagrant life of mendicants.

"Subsequently, O monks, Bhagavat Mahabhignagnanabhibhu, the Tathagata, viewing the prayer of those novices at the lapse of twenty thousand Eons, amply and completely revealed the Dharmaparyaya called 'the Lotus of the True Dharma', a text of great extent, serving to instruct Bodhisattvas and proper for all Buddhas in presence of all the four classes of auditors.

"In course of time, O monks, those sixteen novices grasped, kept, and fully penetrated Bhagavat's teaching.

"Subsequently, O monks, Bhagavat Mahabhignagnanabhibhu, the Tathagata, foretold those sixteen novices their future destiny to supreme, perfect enlightenment. And while Bhagavat Mahabhignagnanabhibhu, the Tathagata, was propounding the Dharmaparyaya of the Lotus of the True Dharma, the disciples as well as the sixteen novices were full of faith, and many hundred thousand myriads of kotis of beings acquired perfect certainty.

"Thereupon, O monks, after propounding the Dharmaparyaya of the Lotus of the True Dharma during eight thousand Eons without interruption, Bhagavat Mahabhignagnanabhibhu, the Tathagata, entered the monastery to retire for the purpose of meditation, and in that retirement, monks, the Tathagata continued in the monastery during eighty-four thousand kotis of Eons.

"Now, monks, when the sixteen novices perceived that Bhagavat was absorbed, they sat down on the seats, the royal thrones which had been prepared for each of them, and amply expounded during eighty-four hundred thousand myriads of kotis the Dharmaparyaya of the Lotus of the True Dharma to the four classes. By doing this each of those novices, as Bodhisattvas fully developed, instructed, excited, stimulated, edified, confirmed in respect to supreme, perfect enlightenment for 60 x 60 hundred thousand myriads of kotis of living beings, equal to the sands of the river Ganges.

"Now, O monks, at the lapse of eighty-four thousand Eons Bhagavat Mahabhignagnanabhibhu, the Tathagata, rose from his meditation, in possession of memory and consciousness, whereafter he went up to the seat of the law designed for him, in order to occupy it.

"As soon as Bhagavat had occupied the seat of the law, O monks, he cast his looks over the whole circle of the audience and addressed the congregation of monks: 'They are wonderfully gifted, monks, they are prodigiously gifted, these sixteen novices, wise, servitors to many hundred thousand myriads of kotis of Buddhas, observers of the course of duty, who have received Buddha-knowledge, transmitted Buddha-knowledge, expounded Buddha-knowledge. Honour these sixteen novices, monks, again and again; and all, be they devoted to the vehicle of the disciples, the vehicle of the Pratyekabuddhas, or the vehicle of the Bodhisattvas, who shall not reject nor repudiate the preaching of these young men of good family, O monks, shall quickly gain supreme, perfect enlightenment, and obtain Tathagata-knowledge.'

"In the sequel also, O monks, have these young men of good family repeatedly revealed this Dharmaparyaya of the Lotus, of the True Dharma under the mastership of that Leader. And the 60 x 60 hundred thousand myriads of kotis of living beings, equal to the sands of the river Ganges, who by each of the sixteen novices, the Bodhisattvas Mahasattvas, in the quality of Bodhisattva, had been roused to enlightenment, all those beings followed the example of the sixteen novices in choosing along with them the vagrant life of mendicants, in their several existences; they enjoyed their sight and heard the law from their mouth. They propitiated forty kotis of Buddhas, and some are doing so up to this day.

"I announce to you, O monks, I declare to you: 'Those sixteen princes, the youths, who as novices under the mastership of Bhagavat were interpreters of the law, have all reached supreme, perfect enlightenment, and all of them are staying, existing, living even now, in the several directions of space, in different Buddha-fields, preaching the law to many hundred thousand myriads of kotis of disciples and Bodhisattvas: in the east, in the world Abhirati is the Tathagata named Akshobhya, the Arhat, and the Tathagata Merukuta, the Arhat; in the south-east, monks, is the Tathagata Simhaghosha and the Tathagata Simhadhvaga; in the south is the Tathagata named Akasapratishthita and the Tathagata named Nityaparinirvrita; in the southwest is the Tathagata named Indradhvaga and the Tathagata named Brahmadhvaga; in the west is the Tathagata named Amitayus and the Tathagata named Sarvalokadhatupadravodvegapratyuttirna; in the north-west is the Tathagata named Tamalapatrakandanagandhabhigna and the Tathagata Merukalpa; in the north is the Tathagata named Meghasvarapradipa and the Tathagata named Meghasvараraga, in the north-east is the Tathagata named Sarvalokabhayagitakkhambhitatvavidhvamsanakara, the Arhat, and, the sixteenth, myself, Sakyamuni, the Tathagata, the Arhat, who have attained supreme, perfect enlightenment in the centre of this Saha-world.

"Further, O monks, those beings who have heard the law from us when we were novices, those many hundred thousand myriads of kotis of beings, numerous as the sands of the river Ganges, whom we have severally initiated in supreme, perfect enlightenment, they are up to this day standing on the stage of disciples and matured for supreme, perfect enlightenment. In regular turn they are to attain supreme, perfect enlightenment, for it is difficult, O monks, to penetrate the knowledge of the Tathagatas. And which are those beings, O monks, who, innumerable, incalculable like the sands of the Ganges, those hundred thousands of myriads of kotis of living beings, whom I, when I was a Bodhisattva under the mastership of that Lord, have taught the law of omniscience? You yourselves, O monks, were at that time those beings.

"And those who shall be my disciples in future, when I shall have attained complete Nirvana, shall learn the course of duty of Bodhisattvas, without conceiving the idea of their being Bodhisattvas. And, monks, all who shall have the idea of complete Nirvana, shall reach it. It should be added, O monks, as I stay under different names in other worlds, they shall there be born again seeking after the knowledge of the Tathagatas, and there they shall anew hear this dogma: 'The complete Nirvana of the Tathagatas is but one; there is no other, no second Nirvana of the Tathagatas.' Herein, monks, one has to see a device of the Tathagatas and a direction for the preaching of the law. When the Tathagata, O monks, knows that the moment of his complete extinction has arrived, and sees that the assemblage is pure, strong in faith, penetrated with the law of voidness, devoted to meditation, devoted to great meditation, then, monks, the Tathagata, because the time has arrived, calls together all Bodhisattvas and all disciples to teach them thus: 'There is, O monks, in this world no second vehicle at all, no second Nirvana, far less a third.' It is an able device of the Tathagata, monks, that on seeing creatures far advanced on the path of perdition, delighting in the low and plunged in the mud of sensual desires, the Tathagata teaches them that Nirvana to which they are attached.

"By way of example, O monks, suppose there is some dense forest five hundred yoganas in extent which has been reached by a great company of men. They have a guide to lead them on their journey to the Isle of

Jewels, which guide, being able, clever, sagacious, well acquainted with the difficult passages of the forest, is to bring the whole company out of the forest. Meanwhile that great troop of men, tired, weary, afraid, and anxious, say: 'Verily, Master, guide, and leader, know that we are tired, weary, afraid, and anxious; let us return; this dense forest stretches so far.' The guide, who is a man of able devices, on seeing those people desirous of returning, thinks to himself: 'It ought not to be that these poor creatures should not reach that great Isle of Jewels. Therefore out of pity for them he makes use of an artifice.' In the middle of that forest he produces a magic city more than a hundred or two hundred yoganas in extent. Thereafter he says to those men: 'Be not afraid, do not return. There you see a populous place where you may take repose and perform all you have to do; there stay in the enjoyment of happy rest. Let him who after reposing there wants to do so, proceed to the great Isle of Jewels.'

"Then, monks, the men who are in the forest are struck with astonishment, and think: 'We are out of the forest; we have reached the place of happy rest; let us stay here.' They enter that magic city, in the meaning that they have arrived at the place of their destination, that they are saved and in the enjoyment of rest. They think: 'We are at rest, we are refreshed'. After a while, when the guide perceives that their fatigue is gone, he causes the magic city to disappear, and says to them: 'Come! There you see the great Isle of Jewels quite near; as to this great city, it has been produced by me for no other purpose but to give you some repose.'

"In the same manner, O monks, is the Tathagata, the Arhat, your guide, and the guide of all other beings. Indeed, monks, the Tathagata, reflects thus: 'Great is this forest of evils which must be crossed, left, shunned. It ought not to be that these beings, after hearing the Buddha-knowledge, should suddenly turn back and not proceed to the end because they think that this Buddha-knowledge is attended with too many difficulties to be gone through to the end.' Under those circumstances the Tathagata, knowing the creatures to be feeble of character, does as the guide who produces the magic city in order that those people may have repose, and after their having taken repose, he tells them that the city is one produced by magic. In the same manner, monks, the Tathagata, to give a repose to the creatures, very skilfully teaches and proclaims two stages of Nirvana: the stage of the disciples and that of the Pratyekabuddhas. And, O monks, when the creatures are there halting, then the Tathagata, himself, pronounces these words: 'You have not accomplished your task, O monks, you have not finished what you had to do. But behold! The Buddha-knowledge is near; behold and be convinced that what to you seems Nirvana, that is not Nirvana.' Nay, O monks, it is an able device of the Tathagatas, that they expound three vehicles."

And in order to explain this same subject more in detail, Bhagavat on that occasion uttered the following stanzas:

60. The Leader of the world, Abhignagnanabhibhu, having occupied the terrace of enlightenment, continued ten complete intermediate kalpas without gaining enlightenment, though he saw the things in their very essence.

61. Then the gods, Nagas, demons, and goblins, zealous to honour the Jina, sent down a rain of flowers on the spot where the Leader awakened to enlightenment.

62. And high in the sky they beat the cymbals to worship and honour the Jina, and they were vexed that the Jina delayed so long in coming to the highest place.

63. After the lapse of ten intermediate kalpas Bhagavat Anabhibhu attained enlightenment. Then all gods, men, serpents, and demons were glad and overjoyed.

64. The sixteen sons of the Leader of men, those heroes, being at the time young princes, rich in virtues, came along with thousands of kotis of

living beings to honour the eminent chiefs of men.

65. And after saluting the feet of the Leader they prayed: 'Reveal the law and refresh us as well as this world with your good word, O Lion amongst kings.

66. 'After a long time you are seen again in the ten points of this world; you appeared, great Leader, while the aerial cars of the Brahma-angels are stirring to reveal a token to living beings.'

67. In the eastern quarter fifty thousand kotis of fields have been shaken, and the lofty angelic cars in them have become excessively brilliant.

68. The Brahma-angels on perceiving this foretoken went and approached the Chief of the Leaders of the world, and, covering him with flowers, presented all of them their cars to him.

69. They prayed him to move forward the wheel of the law, and celebrated him with stanzas and songs. But the king of kings was silent for he thought: 'The time has not yet arrived for me to proclaim the law.'

70. Likewise in the south, west, north, the nadir, zenith, and in the intermediate points of the compass there were thousands of kotis of Brahma-angels.

71. Unremittingly covering Bhagavat with flowers they saluted the feet of the Leader, presented all their aerial cars, celebrated him, and again prayed:

72. 'Move forward the wheel, O you whose sight is infinite! Rarely are you met in the course of many kotis of Eons. Display the benevolence you have observed in so many former generations; open the gate of immortality.'

73. On hearing their prayer, he whose sight is infinite exposed the

multifarious law and the four Truth, saying: 'All existences spring successively from their antecedents.'

74. Starting from ignorance, the Seer proceeded to speak of death, endless woe; all those evils spring from birth. Know likewise that death is the lot of mankind.

75. No sooner had he expounded the multifarious, different, endless laws, than eighty myriads of kotis of creatures who had heard them quickly attained the stage of disciples.

76. On a second occasion the Jina expounded many laws, and beings like the sands of the Ganges became instantly purified and disciples.

77. From that moment the assembly of that Leader of the world was innumerable; no man would be able to reach the term of its number, even were he to go on counting for myriads of kotis of Eons.

78. Those sixteen princes also, his own dear sons, who had become mendicants and novices, said to the Jina: 'Expound, O Chief, the superior law;

79. 'That we may become sages, knowers of the world, such as you are, O supreme of all Jinas, and that all these beings may become such as you are, O Hero, O clear-sighted one.'

80. And the Jina, considering the wish of his sons, the young princes, explained the highest superior enlightenment by means of many myriads of kotis of illustrations.

81. Demonstrating with thousands of arguments and elucidating the knowledge of transcendent wisdom, Bhagavat of the world indicated the veritable course of duty such as was followed by the wise Bodhisattvas.

82. This very Sutra of great extension, this Lotus of the True Dharma, was by Bhagavat delivered in many thousands of stanzas, so numerous as to equal the sands of the Ganges.

83. After delivering this Sutra, the Jina entered the monastery for the purpose of becoming absorbed in meditation; during eighty-four complete Eons Bhagavat of the world continued meditating, sitting on the same seat.

84. Those novices, perceiving that the Chief remained in the monastery without coming out of it, imparted to many kotis of creatures that Buddha-knowledge, which is free from imperfections and blissful.

85. On the seats which they had made to be prepared, one for each, they expounded this very Sutra under the mastership of the Buddha of that period. A service of the same kind they render to me.

86. Innumerable as the sands of sixty thousand rivers like the Ganges were the beings then taught; each of the sons of the Buddha trained endless beings.

87. After the Jina's complete Nirvana they commenced a wandering life and saw kotis of Buddhas; along with those pupils they rendered homage to the most exalted amongst men.

88. Having observed the extensive and sublime course of duty and reached enlightenment in the ten points of space, those sixteen sons of the Jina became themselves Jinas, two by two, in each point of the horizon.

89. And all those who had been their pupils became disciples of those Jinas, and gradually obtained possession of enlightenment by various means.

90. I myself was one of their number, and you have all been taught by me. Therefore you are my disciples now also, and I lead you all to enlightenment by my devices.

91. This is the cause dating from old, this is the motive of my expounding the law, that I lead you to superior enlightenment. This being the case, O monks, you need not be afraid.

92. It is as if there were a forest dreadful, terrific, barren, without a place of refuge or shelter, replete with wild beasts, deprived of water, frightful for persons of no experience.

93. Suppose further that many thousand men have come to the forest, that waste track of wilderness which is fully five hundred yoganas in extent.

94. And he who is to act as their guide through that rough and horrible forest is a rich man, thoughtful, intelligent, wise, well instructed, and undaunted.

95. And those beings, numbering many kotis, feel tired, and say to the guide: 'We are tired, O Master. We are not able to go on and we should like now to return.'

96. But he, the dexterous and clever guide, is searching in his mind for some apt device. Alas! He thinks: 'By going back these foolish men will be deprived of the possession of the jewels.

97. 'Therefore let me by dint of magic power now produce a great city adorned with thousands of kotis of buildings and embellished by monasteries and parks.

98. 'Let me produce ponds and canals; a city adorned with gardens and flowers, provided with walls and gates, and inhabited by an infinite number of men and women.'

99. After creating that city he speaks to them in this manner: 'Do not fear, and be cheerful. You have reached a most excellent city; enter it and do

your business, quickly.

100. 'Be joyful and at ease. You have reached the limit of the whole forest.' It is to give them a time for repose that he speaks these words, and, in fact, they recover from their weariness.

101. As he perceives that they have sufficiently reposed, he collects them and addresses them again: 'Come, hear what I have to tell you. This city have I produced by magic.

102. 'On seeing you fatigued, I have, lest you should go back, made use of this device. Now strain your energy to reach the Isle.'

103. In the same manner, O monks, I am the guide, the conductor of thousands of kotis of living beings; in the same manner I see creatures toiling and unable to break the shell of the egg of evils.

104. Then I reflect on this matter: 'These beings have enjoyed repose, have been tranquillized; now I will remind them of the misery of all things by saying that at the stage of Arhat they shall reach their aim.'

105. At that time, when you shall have attained that state, and when I see all of you have become Arhats, then will I call you all together and explain to you how the law really is.

106. It is an artifice of the Leaders, when they, the great Seers, show three vehicles, for there is but one vehicle, no second, it is only to help creatures that two vehicles are spoken of.

107. Therefore I now tell you, O monks! Rouse to the utmost your lofty energy for the sake of the knowledge of the all-knowing; as yet, you have not come so far as to possess complete Nirvana.

108. But when you shall have attained the knowledge of the all-knowing and the ten powers proper to Jinas, you shall become Buddhas marked by the thirty-two characteristic signs and have rest forever.

109. Such is the teaching of the Leaders: in order to give quiet they speak of repose, but when they see that the creatures have had a repose, they, knowing this to be no final resting-place, initiate them in the knowledge of the all-knowing.

PART VIII.

ANNOUNCEMENT OF THE FUTURE DESTINY OF THE FIVE HUNDRED MONKS

On hearing from Bhagavat that display of skilfulness and the instruction by means of mysterious speech; on hearing the announcement of the future destiny of the great Disciples, as well as the foregoing tale concerning ancient devotion and the leadership of Bhagavat, the venerable Purna, son of Maitrayani, was filled with wonder and amazement, thrilled with pure-heartedness, a feeling of delight and joy. He rose from his seat, full of delight and joy, full of great respect for the law, and while prostrating himself before Bhagavat's feet, made within himself the following reflection: "Wonderful, O Bhagavat! Wonderful, O Buddha! It is an extremely difficult thing that the Tathagatas perform the conforming to this world, composed of so many elements, and preach the law to all creatures with many proofs of their skilfulness, and skilfully release them when attached to this or that. What could we do, O Bhagavat, in such a case? None but the Tathagata knows our inclination and our ancient course." Then, after saluting with his head Bhagavat's feet, Parna went and stood apart, gazing up to Bhagavat with unmoved eyes and so showing his veneration.

And Bhagavat, regarding the mental disposition of the venerable Purna, son of Maitrayani, addressed the entire assembly of monks in this strain: "O monks, see this disciple, Purna, son of Maitrayani, whom I have designated as the foremost of preachers in this assembly, praised for his many virtues, and who has applied himself in various ways to comprehend the true law. He is the man to excite, arouse, and stimulate the four classes of the audience; unwearied in the preaching of the law; as capable to preach the law as to oblige his fellow-followers of the course of duty. The Tathagata excepted, O monks, there is none able to equal Purna, son of Maitrayani, either essentially or in accessories. Now, do you suppose that he keeps my true law only? No, O monks, you must not think so. For I remember, monks, that in the past, in the times of the ninety-nine Buddhas, the same Purna kept the true law under the mastership of those Buddhas. Even as he is now with me, so he has, in all periods, been the foremost of the preachers of the law; has in all periods been a consummate knower of Voidness; has in all periods acquired the four distinctive qualifications of an Arhat; has in all periods reached mastership in the transcendent wisdom of the Bodhisattvas. He has been a strongly convinced preacher of the law, exempt from doubt, and quite pure. Under the mastership of those Buddhas he has during his whole existence observed a spiritual life, and everywhere they termed him 'the Disciple.' By this means he has promoted the interest of innumerable, incalculable hundred thousands of myriads of kotis of beings, and brought innumerable and incalculable beings to full ripeness for supreme and perfect enlightenment. In all periods he has assisted the creatures in the function of a Buddha, and in all periods he has purified his own Buddha-fields, always striving to bring creatures to ripeness. He was also, O monks, the foremost among the preachers of the law under the seven Tathagatas, the first of whom is Vipasyin and the seventh myself.

"And as to the Buddhas, O monks, who have in future to appear in this Bhadra-kalpa, to the number of a thousand less four, under the mastership of them also shall this same Purna, son of Maitrayani, be the foremost among the preachers of the law and the keeper of the true law. Thus he shall keep the true law of innumerable and incalculable Leaders and Buddhas in future, promote the interest of innumerable and incalculable beings, and bring innumerable and incalculable beings to full ripeness for supreme and perfect enlightenment. Constantly and assiduously he shall be instant in purifying his own Buddha-fields and bringing creatures to ripeness. After completing such a Bodhisattva-course, at the end of innumerable, incalculable Eons, he shall reach supreme and perfect enlightenment; he shall in the world be the Tathagata called Dharmaprabhasa, an Arhat, endowed with science and conduct, a Buddha. He shall appear in this very Buddha-fields.

"Further, O monks, at that time the Buddha-fields spoken of will look as if formed by thousands of spheres similar to the sands of the river Ganges. It will be even, like the palm of the hand, consist of seven precious substances, be without hills, and filled with high edifices of seven precious substances. There will be cars of the gods stationed in the sky; the gods will behold men, and men will behold the gods. Moreover, O monks, at that time that Buddha-fields shall be exempt from places of punishment and from womankind, as all beings shall be born by apparitional birth. They shall lead a spiritual life, have ideal bodies, be self-lighting, magical, moving in the firmament, strenuous, of good memory, wise, possessed of gold-coloured bodies, and adorned with the thirty-two characteristics of a great man. And at that time the beings in that Buddha-fields will have two things to feed upon: the delight in the law and the delight in meditation. There will be an immense, incalculable number of hundred thousands of myriads of kotis of Bodhisattvas; all endowed with great transcendent wisdom, accomplished in the four distinctive qualifications of an Arhat, able in instructing creatures. He, that Buddha, will have a number of disciples, beyond all calculation, mighty in magic, powerful, masters in the meditation of the eight emancipations. So immense are the good qualities that Buddha-fields will be possessed of. And that Eon shall be called Ratnavabhasa (Radiant with gems), and that world Suvisuddha (Very pure). His lifetime shall last immense incalculable Eons; and after the complete extinction of that Lord Dharmaprabhasa, the Tathagata, his true law shall last long, and his world shall be full of Stupas made of precious substances. Such inconceivable good qualities, O monks, shall the Buddha-fields of that Buddha be possessed of.

So spoke Bhagavat, and thereafter he, the Buddha, the Master, added the following stanzas:

1. Listen to me, O monks, and hear how my son has achieved his course of duty, and how he, well trained and skilful, has observed the course of enlightenment.

2. Viewing these beings to be lowly-disposed and to be startled at the lofty vehicle, the Bodhisattvas become disciples and exercise Pratyekabuddhaship.

3. By many hundreds of able devices they bring numerous Bodhisattvas to full ripeness and declare: 'We are but disciples, indeed, and we are far away from the highest and supreme enlightenment.'

4. It is by learning from them this course of duty that kotis of beings arrive at full ripeness, who at first lowly-disposed and somewhat lazy, in course of time all become Buddhas.

5. They follow a course in ignorance thinking: 'We, disciples, are of little use, indeed! In despondency they descend into all places of existence successively, and so clear their own field.

6. They show in their own persons that they are not free from affection, hatred, and infatuation; and on perceiving other beings clinging to heretical views, they go so far as to accommodate themselves to those views.

7. By following such a course my numerous disciples skilfully save creatures; simple people would go mad, if they were taught the whole course of life or story.

8. Purna here, monks, my disciple, has formerly fulfilled his course of duty under thousands of kotis of Buddhas, he has got possession of this true law by seeking after Buddha-knowledge.

9. And at all periods has he been the foremost of the disciples, learned, a brilliant orator, free from hesitation; he has, indeed, always been able to excite to gladness and at all times ready to perform the Buddha-task.

10. He has always been accomplished in the sublime transcendent faculties and endowed with the distinctive qualifications of an Arhat; he knew the faculties and range of other beings, and has always preached the perfectly pure law.

11. By exposing the most eminent of true laws he has brought thousands of kotis of beings to full ripeness for this supreme, foremost vehicle, whilst purifying his own excellent field.

12. In future also he shall likewise honour thousands of kotis of Buddhas, acquire knowledge of the most eminent of good laws, and clean his own field.

13. Always free from timidity he shall preach the law with thousands of kotis of able devices, and bring many beings to full ripeness for the knowledge of the all-knowing that is free from imperfections.

14. After having paid homage to the Leaders of men and always kept the most eminent of laws, he shall in the world be a Buddha self-born, widely renowned everywhere by the name of Dharmaprabhasa.

15. And his field shall always be very pure and always set off with seven precious substances; his Eon shall be called Ratnavabhasa, and his world Suvisuddha.

16. That world shall be pervaded with many thousand kotis of Bodhisattvas, accomplished masters in the great transcendent sciences, pure in every respect, and endowed with magical power.

17. At that period the Leader shall also have an assemblage of thousands of kotis of disciples, endowed with magical power, adepts at the meditation of the eight emancipations, and accomplished in the four distinctive qualifications of an Arhat.

18. And all beings in that Buddha-fields shall be pure and lead a spiritual life. Springing into existence by apparitional birth, they shall all be gold coloured and display the thirty-two characteristic signs.

19. They shall know no other food but pleasure in the law and delight in knowledge. No womankind shall be there, nor fear of the places of punishments or of dismal states.

20. Such shall be the excellent field of Purna, who is possessed of all good qualities; it shall abound with all goodly things, a small part only of which has here been mentioned.

Then this thought arose in the mind of those twelve hundred self-controlled Arhats: "We are struck with wonder and amazement. How if the Tathagata would predict to us severally our future destiny as Bhagavat has done to those other great disciples?"

And Bhagavat apprehending in his own mind what was going on in the minds of these great disciples addressed the venerable Maha-Kasyapa: "Those twelve hundred self-controlled hearers whom I am now beholding from face to face, to all those twelve hundred self-controlled hearers, Kasyapa, I will presently foretell their destiny. Amongst them, Kasyapa, the monk Kaundinya, a great disciple, shall, after sixty-two hundred thousand myriads of kotis of Buddhas, become a Tathagata, an Arhat, under the name of

Samantaprabhasa, endowed with science and conduct, a Buddha; but of those twelve hundred, Kasyapa, five hundred shall become Tathagatas of the same name. Thereafter shall all those five hundred great disciples reach supreme and perfect enlightenment, all bearing the name of Samantaprabhasa: Gaya-Kasyapa, Nadi-Kasyapa, Uruvilva.-Kasyapa, Kala, KaIodayin, Aniruddha, Kapphina, Vakkula, Kunda, Svagata, and the rest of the five hundred self-controlled Arhats."

And on that occasion Bhagavat uttered the following stanzas:

21. The scion of the Kundina family, my disciple here, shall in future be a Tathagata, a Leader of the world, after the lapse of an endless period; he shall educate hundreds of kotis of living beings.

22. After seeing many endless Buddhas, he shall in future, after the lapse of an endless period, become the Jina Samantaprabhasa, whose field shall be thoroughly pure.

23. Brilliant, gifted with the powers of a Buddha, with a voice far resounding in all quarters, waited upon by thousands of kotis of beinas, he shall preach supreme and eminent enlightenment.

24. There shall be most zealous Bodhisattvas, mounted on lofty aereal cars, and moving, meditative, pure in morals, and assiduous in doing good.

25. After hearing the law from the highest of men, they shall invariably go to other fields, to salute thousands of Buddhas and show them great honour.

26. But before long they shall return to the field of the Leader called Prabhasa, the Tathagata. So great shall be the power of their course of duty.

27. The measure of the lifetime of that Buddha shall be sixty thousand Eons, and, after the complete extinction of that mighty one, his true law

shall remain twice as long in the world.

28. And the counterfeit of it shall continue three times as long. When the true law of that holy one shall he exhausted, men and gods shall be vexed.

29. There shall appear a complete number of five hundred Leaders, supreme amongst men, who shall bear the same name with that Jina, Samantaprabha, and follow one another in regular succession.

30. All shall have like divisions, magical powers, Buddha-fields, and hosts of followers. Their true law also shall be the same and stand equally long.

31. All shall have in this world, including the gods, the same voice as Samantaprabha, the highest of men, such as I have mentioned before.

32. Moved by benevolence and compassion they shall in succession foretell each other's destiny with the words: 'This is to be my immediate successor, and he is to command the world as I do at present.'

33. Thus, Kasyapa, keep now in view these self-controlled Arhats here, no less than five hundred in number, as well as my other disciples, and speak of this matter to the other disciples.

On hearing from Bhagavat the announcement of their own future destiny, the five hundred Arhats, contented, satisfied, in high spirits and ecstasy, filled with cheerfulness, joy, and delight, went up to the place where Bhagavat was sitting, reverentially saluted with their heads his feet, and spoke thus: "We confess our fault, O Bhagavat, in having continually and constantly persuaded ourselves that we had arrived at final Nirvana, as persons who are dull, inept, ignorant of the rules, For, O Bhagavat, whereas we should have thoroughly penetrated the knowledge of the Tathagatas, we were content with such a trifling degree of knowledge.

"It is, O Bhagavat, as if some man having come to a friend's house got drunk or fell asleep, and that friend bound a priceless gem within his garment, with the thought: 'Let this gem be his.' After a while, O Bhagavat, that man rises from his seat and travels further; he goes to some other country, where he is befallen by incessant difficulties, and has great trouble to find food and clothing. By dint of great exertion he is hardly able to obtain a bit of food, with which he is contented and satisfied. The old friend of that man, O Bhagavat, who bound within the man's garment that priceless gem, happens to see him again and says: 'How is it, good friend, that you have such difficulty in seeking food and clothing, while I, in order that you should live in ease, good friend, have bound within your garment a priceless gem, quite sufficient to fulfil all your wishes? I have given you that gem, my good friend, the very gem I have bound within your garment. Still you are deliberating what has been bound, by whom and for what reason. It is something foolish, my good friend, to be contented, when you have with so much difficulty to procure food and clothing. Go, my good friend, betake yourself, with this gem, to some great city, exchange the gem for money, and with that money do all that can be done with money.'

"In the same manner, O Bhagavat, has the Tathagata formerly, when he still followed the course of duty of a Bodhisattva, raised in us also ideas of omniscience, but we, O Bhagavat, did not perceive, nor know it. We fancied, O Bhagavat, that on the stage of Arhat we had reached Nirvana. We live in difficulty, O Bhagavat, because we content ourselves with such a trifling degree of knowledge. But as our strong aspiration after the knowledge of the all-knowing has never ceased, the Tathagata teaches us the right: 'Have no such idea of Nirvana, O monks. There are in your intelligence roots of goodness which of long ago I have fully developed. In this you have to see an able device of mine that from the expressions used by me, in preaching the law, you fancy Nirvana to take place at this moment.' And after having taught us the right in such a way, Bhagavat now predicts our future destiny to supreme and perfect knowledge."

And on that occasion the five hundred self-controlled Arhats, Agnata-Kaundinya and the rest, uttered the following stanzas:

34. We are rejoicing and delighted to hear this unsurpassed word of comfort that we are destined to the highest, supreme enlightenment. Homage be to you, O Bhagavat of unlimited sight!

35. We confess our fault before you; we were so childish, nescient, ignorant that we were fully contented with a small part of Nirvana, under the mastership of the Buddha.

36. This is a case like that of a certain man who enters the house of a friend, which friend, being rich and wealthy, gives him much food, both hard and soft.

37. After satiating him with nourishment, he gives him a jewel of great value. He ties it with a knot within the upper robe and feels satisfaction at having given that jewel.

38. The other man, unaware of it, goes forth and from that place travels to another town. There he is befallen with misfortune and, as a miserable beggar, seeks his food in affliction.

39. He is contented with the pittance he gets by begging without caring for dainty food; as to that jewel, he has forgotten it; he has not the slightest remembrance of its having been tied in his upper robe.

40. Under these circumstances he is seen by his old friend who at home gave him that jewel. This friend properly reprimands him and shows him the jewel within his robe.

41. At this sight the man feels extremely happy. The value of the jewel is such that he becomes a very rich man, of great power, and in possession of

all that the five senses can enjoy.

42. In the same manner, O Bhagavat, we were unaware of our former aspiration, the aspiration laid in us by the Tathagata himself in previous existences from time immemorial.

43. And we were living in this world, O Bhagavat, with dull understanding and in ignorance, under the mastership of the Buddha; for we were contented with a little of Nirvana; we required nothing higher, nor even cared for it.

44. But the Friend of the world has taught us better: 'This is no blessed Rest at all; the full knowledge of the highest men, that is blessed Rest, that is supreme beatitude."

45. After hearing this sublime, grand, splendid, and matchless prediction, O Bhagavat, we are greatly elated with joy, when thinking of the prediction we shall have to make to each other in regular succession.

PART IX.

ANNOUNCEMENT OF THE FUTURE DESTINY OF ANANDA, RAHULA, AND THE TWO THOUSAND MONKS

On that occasion the venerable Ananda made this reflection: "Should we also receive a similar prediction?" Thus thinking, pondering, wishing, he rose from his seat, prostrated himself at Bhagavat's feet and uttered the following words. And the venerable Rahula also, in whom rose the same thought and the same wish as in Ananda, prostrated himself at Bhagavat's feet, and uttered these words: "Let it be our turn also, O Bhagavat. Let it be our turn also, O Buddha. Bhagavat is our father and procreator, our refuge and protection. For in this world, including men, gods, and demons, O Bhagavat, we are particularly distinguished, as people say: 'These are Bhagavat's sons, Bhagavat's attendants; these are the keepers of the law-treasure of Bhagavat.' Therefore, it would seem proper, if Bhagavat before long could predict our destiny to supreme and perfect enlightenment."

Two thousand other monks, and more, both such as were still under training and such as were not, likewise rose from their seats, put their upper robes upon one shoulder, stretched their joined hands towards Bhagavat and remained gazing up to him, all pre-occupied with the same thought of this very Buddha-knowledge: "Should we also receive a prediction of our destiny to supreme and perfect enlightenment?"

Then Bhagavat addressed the venerable ananda in these words: "You, Ananda, shall in future become a Tathagata by the name of Sagaravarad-harabuddhivikriditabhigna, an Arhat, endowed with science and conduct. After having honoured, respected, venerated, and worshipped sixty-two kotis of Buddhas, kept in memory the true law of those Buddhas and received this command, you shall arrive at supreme and perfect enlightenment, and bring to full ripeness for supreme, perfect enlightenment twenty hundred thousand myriads of kotis of Bodhisattvas similar to the sands of twenty Ganges. And your Buddha-fields shall consist of lapis lazuli and be superabundant. The sphere shall be named Anavanamita-vaig-ayanta and the Eon Manognasabdabhigargita. The lifetime of that Leader Sagaravaradharabuddhivikriditabhigna, the Tathagata, shall measure an immense number of Eons, Eons the term of which is not to be found by calculation. So many hundred thousand myriads of kotis of incalculable Eons shall last the lifetime of that Lord. Twice as long, Ananda, after the complete extinction of that Buddha, shall his true law stand, and twice as long again shall continue its counterfeit. And further, Ananda, many hundred thousand myriads of kotis of Buddhas, similar to the sands of the river Ganges, shall in all directions of space speak the praise of that Tathagata Sagaravaradharabuddhivikriditabhigna, the Arhat.

1. I announce to you, O monks, that Ananda-Bhadra, the keeper of my law,

shall in future become a Jina, after having worshipped sixty kotis of Buddhas.

2. He shall be widely renowned by the name of Sagarabuddhidharin Abhignaprapta (Possessor of an intellect unfathomable as the ocean, having arrived at transcendant wisdom) in a beautiful, thoroughly clear Buddha-field Anavanata Vaigayanti (Triumphal banner unlowered).

3. There shall be Bodhisattvas like the sands of the Ganges and even more, whom he shall bring to full ripeness; he shall be a Jina endowed with great magical power, whose word shall widely resound in all quarters of the world.

4. The duration of his life shall be immense. He shall always be benign and merciful to the world. After the complete extinction of that Jina and mighty saint Tayin, his true law shall stand twice as long.

5. The counterfeit shall continue twice as long under the rule of that Jina. Then also shall beings like grains of sand of the Ganges produce in this world what is the cause of Buddha-enlightenment.

In that assembly were eight thousand Bodhisattvas who had newly entered the vehicle. To them this thought presented itself: 'Never before did we have such a sublime prediction to Bodhisattvas, far less to disciples. What may be the cause of it? What the motive?'

Bhagavat, who apprehended in his mind what was going on in the minds of those Bodhisattvas, addressed them in these words: "Young men of good family, I and Ananda have in the same moment, the same instant conceived the idea of supreme and perfect enlightenment in the presence of the Tathagata Dharmagahanabhyudgataraga, the Arhat. At that period, young men of good family, Ananda constantly and assiduously applied himself to great learning, whereas I was applying myself to strenuous labour. Hence I sooner arrived at supreme and perfect enlightenment, whilst Ananda-Bhadra was the keeper of the law-treasure of Bhagavats Buddhas. That is to say, young men of good family, he made a vow to bring Bodhisattvas to full development."

When the venerable Ananda, heard from Bhagavat the announcement of his own destiny to supreme and perfect enlightenment, when he learned the good qualities of his Buddha-fields and its divisions, when he heard of the vow he had made in the past, he felt pleased, exultant, ravished, joyous, filled with cheerfulness and delight. And at that juncture he remembered the true law of many hundred thousand rnyriads of kotis of Buddhas and his own vow from long ago.

And on that occasion the venerable Ananda uttered the following stanzas:

6. Wonderful, boundless are the Jinas who remind us of the law preached by the extinct Jinas and mighty saints. Now I remember it as if it had happened today or yesterday.

7. I am freed from all doubts and ready for enlightenment. Such is my skilfulness, as I am the servitor and keep the true law for the sake of enlightenment.

Thereupon Bhagavat addressed the venerable Rahula-Bhadra in these words: "You, Rahula, shall be in future a Tathagata of the name of Saptaratnapadmavikrantagamin, an Arhat, endowed with science and conduct. After having honoured, respected, venerated, worshipped a number of Tathagata, equal to the atoms of ten worlds, you shall always be the eldest son of those Buddhas, just as you are mine at present. And, Rahula, the measure of the lifetime of that Leader Saptaratnapadmavikrantagamin, the Tathagata, and the abundance of all sorts of good qualities belonging to him shall be exactly the same as of Bhagavat Sagaravaradharabuddhivikriditabhigna, the Tathagata. Likewise shall the divisions of the Buddha-fields and its qualities be the same as those possessed by that Lord. And, Rahula, you shall be the eldest son of that

Tathagata Sagaravaradharabuddhivikriditabhigna, the Arhat. Afterwards, you shall arrive at supreme and perfect enlightenment.

8. Rahula here, my own eldest son, who was born to me when I was a prince royal, he, my son, after my reaching enlightenment, is a great Seer, an heir to the law.

9. The great number of kotis of Buddhas which he shall see in future, is immense. To all these Jinas he shall be a son, striving after enlightenment.

10. Unknown is this course of duty to Rahula, but I know his former vow. He glorifies the Friend of the world by saying: 'I am, forsooth, the Tathagata's son.'

11. Innumerable myriads of kotis of good qualities, the measure of which is never to be found, appertain to this Rahula, my son, for he exists by reason of enlightenment.

Bhagavat now again regarded those two thousand disciples, both such as were still under training and such as were not, who were looking up to him with serene, mild, placid minds. And Bhagavat then addressed the venerable Ananda: "Do you see, Ananda, these two thousand disciples, both such as are still under training and such as are not?"

Ananda responded: "I do, O Bhagavat; I do, O Buddha."

Bhagavat proceeded: "All these two thousand monks, Ananda, shall simultaneously accomplish the course of Bodhisattvas, and after honouring, respecting, venerating, worshipping Buddhas as numerous as the atoms of fifty worlds, and after acquiring the true law, they shall, in their last bodily existence, attain supreme and perfect enlightenment at the same time, the same moment, the same instant, the same juncture in all directions of space, in different worlds, each in his own Buddha-fields. They shall become

Tathagatas, Arhats, by the name of Ratnaketuragas. Their lifetime shall last a complete Eon. The division and good qualities of their Buddha-fields shall be equal; equal also shall be the number of the congregation of their disciples and Bodhisattvas; equal also shall be their complete extinction, and their true law shall continue an equal time."

And on that occasion Bhagavat uttered the following stanzas:

12. These two thousand disciples, Ananda, who here are standing before me, to them, the sages, I now predict that in future they shall become Tathagatas.

13. After having paid eminent worship to the Buddhas, by means of infinite comparisons and examples, they shall, when standing in their last bodily existence, reach my extreme enlightenment.

14. They shall all, under the same name, in every direction, at the same moment and instant, and sitting at the foot of the most exalted tree, become Buddhas, after they shall have reached the knowledge.

15. All shall bear the same name of Ketus of the Ratna, by which they shall be widely famed in this world. Their excellent fields shall be equal, and equal the congregation of disciples and Bodhisattvas.

16. Strong in magic power, they shall all simultaneously, in every direction of space, reveal the law in this world and all at once become extinct; their true law shall last equally long.

And the disciples, both such as were still under training and such as were not, on hearing from Bhagavat, face to face, the prediction concerning each of them, were pleased, exultant, ravished, joyous, filled with cheerfulness and delight, and addressed Bhagavat with the following stanzas:

17. We are satisfied, O Light of the world, to hear this prediction. We

are pleased, O Tathagata, as if sprinkled with nectar.

18. We have no doubt, no uncertainty that we shall become supreme amongst men; today we have obtained felicity, because we have heard that prediction.

PART X.

THE PREACHER

Bhagavat then addressed the eighty thousand Bodhisattvas Mahasattvas by turning to Bhaishagyaraga as their representative: "Do you see, Bhaishagyaraga, in this assembly the many gods, Nagas, goblins, Gandharvas, demons, Garudas, Kinnaras, great serpents, men, and beings not human, monks, nuns, male and female lay devotees, votaries of the vehicle of disciples, votaries of the vehicle of Pratyekabuddhas, and those of the vehicle of Bodhisattvas, who have heard this Dharmaparyaya from the mouth of the Tathagata?"

Bhaishagyaraga responded: "I do, O Bhagavat; I do, O Buddha."

Bhagavat proceeded: "Well, Bhaishagyaraga, all those Bodhisattvas Mahasattvas who in this assembly have heard, were it but a single stanza, a single verse, or who even by a single rising thought have joyfully accepted this Sutra, to all of them, Bhaishagyaraga, among the four classes of my audience I predict their destiny to supreme and perfect enlightenment. And all whosoever, Bhaishagyaraga, who, after the complete extinction of the Tathagata, shall hear this Dharmaparyaya and after hearing, were it but a single stanza, joyfully accept it, even with a single rising thought, to those also, Bhaishagyaraga, be they young men or young ladies of good family, I predict their destiny to supreme and perfect enlightenment. Those young men or ladies of good family, Bhaishagyaraga, shall be worshippers of many hundred thousand myriads of kotis of Buddhas. Those young men or ladies of good family, Bhaishagyaraga, shall have made a vow under hundred thousands of myriads of kotis of Buddhas. They must be considered as being reborn amongst the people of Gambudvipa, out of compassion to all creatures. Those who shall take, read, make known, recite, copy, and after copying always keep in memory and from time to time regard were it but a single stanza of this Dharmaparyaya; who by that book shall feel veneration for the Tathagatas, treat them with the respect due to Masters, honour, revere, worship them; who shall worship that book with flowers, incense, perfumed garlands, ointment, powder, clothes, umbrellas, flags, banners, music, and with acts of reverence such as bowing and joining hands; in short, Bhaishagyaraga, any young men or young ladies of good family who shall keep or joyfully accept were it but a single stanza of this Dharmaparyaya, to all of them, Bhaishagyaraga, I predict their being destined to supreme and perfect enlightenment.

"Should some man or woman, Bhaishagyaraga, happen to ask: 'How now have those creatures to be who in future are to become Tathagatas, Arhats?' Then that man or woman should be referred to the example of that young man or young lady of good family. Whoever is able to keep, recite, or teach, were it but a single stanza of four lines, and whoever shows respect for this Dharmaparyaya, that young man or young lady of good family shall in future become a Tathagata. Be persuaded of it. For, Bhaishagyaraga, such a young man or young lady of good family must be considered to be a Tathagata, and by the whole world, including the gods, honour should be done to such a Tathagata who keeps were it but a single stanza of this Dharmaparyaya, and far more, of course, to one who grasps, keeps, comprehends, makes known, copies, and after copying always retains in his memory this Dharmaparyaya entirely and completely, and who honours that book with flowers, incense, perfumed garlands, ointment, powder, clothes, umbrellas, flags, banners, music, joined hands, reverential bows and salutations. Such a young man or young lady of good family, Bhaishagyaraga, must be held to be accomplished in supreme and perfect enlightenment; must be held to be the like of a Tathagata, who out of compassion and for the benefit of the world, by virtue of a former vow, makes his appearance here in Gambudvipa, in order to make this Dharmaparyaya generally known. Whosoever, after leaving his own lofty conception of the law and the lofty Buddha-fields occupied by him, in order to make generally known this Dharmaparyaya, after my complete Nirvana, may be deemed to have appeared in the predicament of a Tathagata, such a one, Bhaishagyaraga, be it a young man or a young lady of good family, must be held to perform the function of the Tathagata, to be a deputy of the Tathagata. As such, Bhaishagyaraga, should be acknowledged the young man or the young lady of good family, who communicates this Dharmaparyaya, after the complete Nirvana of the Tathagata, were it but in secret or by stealth or to one single creature that he communicated or told it.

"Again, Bhaishagyaraga, if some creature vicious, wicked, and cruel-minded should in the current Age speak something injurious in the face of the Tathagata, and if some should utter a single harsh word, founded or unfounded, to those irreproachable preachers of the law and keepers of this Sutranta, whether lay devotees or clergymen, I declare that the latter sin is the graver. For, Bhaishagyaraga, such a young man or young lady of good family must be held to be adorned with the apparel of the Tathagata. He carries the Tathagata on his shoulder, Bhaishagyaraga, who after having copied this Dharmaparyaya and made a volume of it, carries it on his shoulder. Such a one, wherever he goes, must be saluted by all beings with joined hands, must be honoured, respected, worshipped, venerated, revered by gods and men with flowers, incense, perfumed garlands, ointment, powder, clothes, umbrellas, flags, banners, musical instruments, with food, soft and hard, with nourishment and drink, with vehicles, with heaps of choice and gorgeous jewels. That preacher of the law must be honoured by heaps of gorgeous jewels being presented to that preacher of the law. For it may be that by his expounding this Dharmaparyaya, were it only once, innumerable, incalculable beings who hear it shall soon become accomplished in supreme and perfect enlightenment."

And on that occasion Bhagavat uttered the following stanzas:

1. He who wishes to be established in Buddhahood and aspires to the knowledge of the Self-born must honour those who keep this doctrine.

2. And he who is desirous of omniscience and thinks: 'How shall I soonest reach it?' must try to know this Sutra by heart, or at least honour one who knows it.

3. He has been sent by Bhagavat of the world to educate men, he who out of compassion for mankind recites this Sutra.

4. After giving up a good position, that great man has come hither, he who out of compassion for mankind keeps this Sutra in memory.

5. It is by force of his position, that in the last times he is seen preaching this unsurpassed Sutra.

6. That preacher of the law must be honoured with divine and human flowers and all sorts of perfumes, be decked with divine cloth and strewed with jewels.

7. One should always reverentially salute him with joined hands, as if he were the Chief of Jinas or the Self-born, he who in these most dreadful, last days keeps this Sutra of the Extinct Buddha.

8. One should give food, hard and soft, nourishment and drink, lodging in a convent, kotis of robes to honour the son of Jina, when he has propounded, be it but once, this Sutra.

9. He performs the task of the Tathagatas and has been sent by me to the world of men, he who in the last days shall copy, keep, or hear this Sutra.

10. The man who in wickedness of heart or with frowning brow should at

any time of a whole Eon utter something injurious in my presence, commits a great sin.

11. But one who reviles and abuses those guardians of this Sutra, when they are expounding this Sutra, I say that he commits a still greater sin.

12. The man who, striving for superior enlightenment, shall in a complete Eon praise me in my face with joined hands, with many myriads of kotis of stanzas,

13. Shall as a consequence derive a great merit, since he has glorified me in gladness of heart. But a still greater merit shall he acquire who pronounces the praise of those preachers.

14. One who shall during eighteen thousand kotis of Eons pay worship to those objects of veneration, with words, visible things, flavours, with divine scents and divine kinds of touch,

15. If such a one, by his paying that worship to the objects of veneration during eighteen thousand kotis of Eons, happens to hear this Sutra, were it only once, he shall obtain an amazingly great advantage.

"I announce to you, Bhaishagyaraga, I declare to you, that many are the Dharmaparyayas which I have propounded, am propounding, and shall propound. And among all those Dharmaparyayas, Bhaishagyaraga, it is this which is apt to meet with no acceptance with everybody, to find no belief with everybody. This, indeed, Bhaishagyaraga, is the transcendent spiritual esoteric lore of the law, preserved by the power of the Tathagatas, but never divulged; it is an article of creed not yet made known. By the majority of people, Bhaishagyaraga, this Dharmaparyaya is rejected during the lifetime of the Tathagata; in far higher degree such will be the case after his complete extinction.

"Nevertheless, Bhaishagyaraga, one has to consider those young men or young ladies of good family to be invested with the robes of the Tathagata; to be regarded and blessed by the Tathagatas living in other worlds, that they shall have the force of individual persuasion, the force that is rooted in virtue, and the force of a pious vow. They shall dwell apart in the convents of the Tathagata, Bhaishagyaraga, and shall have their heads stroked by the hand of the Tathagata, those young men and young ladies of good family, who after the complete extinction of the Tathagata shall believe, read, write, honour this Dharmaparyaya and recite it to others.

"Again, Bhaishagyaraga, on any spot of the earth where this Dharmaparyaya is expounded, preached, written, studied, or recited in chorus, on that spot, Bhaishagyaraga, one should build a Tathagata-shrine, magnificent, consisting of precious substances, high, and spacious; but it is not necessary to depose in it relics of the Tathagata. For the body of the Tathagata is, so to say, collectively deposited there. Any spot of the earth where this Dharmaparyaya is expounded or taught or recited or rehearsed in chorus or written or kept in a volume, must be honoured, respected, revered, worshipped as if it were a Stupa, with all sorts of flowers, incense, perfumes, garlands, ointment, powder, clothes, umbrellas, flags, banners, triumphal streamers, with all kinds of song, music, dancing, musical instruments, castanets, and shouts in chorus. And those, Bhaishagyaraga, who approach a Tathagata-shrine to salute or see it, must be held to be near supreme and perfect enlightenment. For, Bhaishagyaraga, there are many laymen as well as priests who observe the course of a Bodhisattva without, however, coming so far as to see, hear, write or worship this Dharmaparyaya. So long as they do not hear this Dharmaparyaya, they are not yet proficient in the course of a Bodhisattva. But those who hear this Dharmaparyaya and thereupon accept, penetrate, understand, comprehend it, are at the time near supreme, perfect enlightenment, so to say, immediately near it.

"It is a case, Bhaishagyaraga, similar to that of a certain man, who in need and in quest of water, in order to get water, causes a well to be dug in an and tract of land. So long as he sees that the sand being dug out is dry and white, he thinks: 'The water is still far off.' After some time he sees that the sand being dug out is moist, mixed with water, muddy, with trickling drops, and that the working men who are engaged in digging the well are bespattered with mire and mud. On seeing that foretoken, Bhaishagyaraga, the man will be convinced and certain that water is near. In the same manner, Bhaishagyaraga, will these Bodhisattvas Mahasattvas be far away from supreme and perfect enlightenment so long as they do not hear, nor catch, nor penetrate, nor fathom, nor mind this Dharmaparyaya. But when the Bodhisattvas Mahasattvas shall hear, catch, penetrate, study, and mind this Dharmaparyaya, then, Bhaishagyaraga, they will be, so to say, immediately near supreme, perfect enlightenment. From this Dharmaparyaya, Bhaishagyaraga, will accrue to creatures supreme and perfect enlightenment. For this Dharmaparyaya contains an explanation of the highest mystery, the secret article of the law which the Tathagatas, have revealed for the perfecting of the Bodhisattvas Mahasattvas. Any Bodhisattva, Bhaishagyaraga, who is startled, feels anxiety, gets frightened at this Dharmaparyaya, may be held, Bhaishagyaraga, to have but newly entered the vehicle. If, however, a votary of the vehicle of the disciples is startled, feels anxiety, gets frightened at this Dharmaparyaya, such a person, devoted to the vehicle of the disciples, Bhaishagyaraga, may be deemed a conceited man.

"Any Bodhisattva Mahasattva, Bhaishagyaraga, who after the complete extinction of the Tathagata, in the last times, the last period shall set forth this Dharmaparyaya to the four classes of hearers, should do so, Bhaishagyariga, after having entered the abode of the Tathagata, after having put on the robe of the Tathagata, and occupied the pulpit of the Tathagata. And what is the abode of the Tathagata, Bhaishagyaraga? It is the abiding in charity and kindness to all beings; that is the abode of the Tathagata, Bhaishagyaraga, which the young man of good family has to enter. And what is the robe of the Tathagata, Bhaishagyaraga? It is the apparel of sublime forbearance; that is the robe of the Tathagata, Bhaishagyaraga, which the young man of good family has to put on. What is the pulpit of the Tathagata,

Bhaishagyaraga? It is the entering into the voidness of all things; that is the pulpit, Bhaishagyaraga, on which the young man of good family has to sit in order to set forth this Dharmaparyaya to the four classes of hearers. A Bodhisattva ought to propound this Dharmaparyaya with unshrinking mind, before the face of the congregated Bodhisattvas, the four classes of hearers, who are striving for the vehicle of Bodhisattvas, and I, staying in another world, Bhaishagyaraga, will by means of fictious creatures make the minds of the whole congregation favourably disposed to that young man of good family, and I will send fictious monks, nuns, male and female lay devotees in order to hear the sermon of the preacher, who are unable to gainsay or contradict him. If afterwards he shall have retired to the forest, I will send thither many gods, Nagas, goblins, Gandharvas, demons, Garudas, Kinnaras, and great serpents to hear him preach, while I, staying in another world, Bhaishagyaraga, will show my face to that young man of good family, and the words and syllables of this Dharmaparyaya which he happens to have forgotten will I again suggest to him when he repeats his lesson."

And on that occasion Bhagavat uttered the following stanzas:

16. Let one listen to this exalted Sutra, avoiding all distractedness; for rare is the occasion given for hearing it, and rare also the belief in it.

17. It is a case similar to that of a certain man who in want of water goes to dig a well in an arid tract of land, and sees how again and again only dry sand is being dug up.

18. On seeing which he thinks: 'The water is far off.' A token of its being far off is the dry white sand which appears in digging.

19. But when he afterwards sees again and again the sand moist and smooth, he gets the conviction that water cannot be very far off.

20. So, too, are those men far from Buddha-knowledge who have not

heard this Sutra and have failed to repeatedly meditate on it.

21. But those who have heard and often meditated on this profound king amongst Sutras, this authoritative book for disciples,

22. Are wise and near Buddha-knowledge, even as from the moisture of sand may be inferred that water is near.

23. After entering the abode of the Jina, putting on his robe and sitting down on my seat, the preacher should, undaunted, expound this Sutra.

24. The strength of charity or kindness is my abode; the apparel of forbearance is my robe; and voidness (abstraction) is my seat; let the preacher take his stand on this and preach.

25. Where clods, sticks, pikes, or abusive words and threats fall to the lot of the preacher, let him be patient, thinking of me.

26. My body has existed entire in thousands of kotis of regions; during a number of kotis of.Eons beyond comprehension I teach the law to creatures.

27. To that courageous man who shall proclaim this Sutra after my complete extinction I will also send many creations.

28. Monks, nuns, lay devotees, male and female, will honour him as well as the classes of the audience.

29. And should there be some to attack him with clods, sticks, injurious words, threats, taunts, then the creations shall defend him.

30. And when he shall stay alone, engaged in study, in a lonely place, in the forest or the hills,

31. Then will I show him my luminous body and enable him to remember the lesson he forgot.

32. While he is living lonely in the wilderness, I will send him gods and goblins in great number to keep him company.

33. Such are the advantages he is to enjoy, whether he is preaching to the four classes, or living, a solitary, in mountain caverns and studying his lesson, he will see me.

34. His readiness of speech knows no impediment; he understands the manifold requisites of exegesis; he satisfies thousands of kotis of beings because he is, so to say, inspired or blessed by the Buddha.

35. And the creatures who are entrusted to his care shall very soon all become Bodhisattvas, and by cultivating his intimacy they shall behold Buddhas as numerous as the sands of the Ganges.

PART XI.

APPARITION OF A STUPA

Then there arose a Stupa, consisting of seven precious substances, from the place of the earth opposite Bhagavat, the assembly being in the middle, a Stupa five hundred yoganas in height and proportionate in circumference. After its rising, the Stupa, a meteoric phenomenon, stood in the sky sparkling, beautiful, nicely decorated with five thousand successive terraces of flowers, adorned with many thousands of arches, embellished by thousands of banners and triumphal streamers, hung with thousands of jewel-garlands and with hour-plates and bells, and emitting the scent of Xanthochymus and sandal, which scent filled this whole world. Its row of umbrellas rose so far on high as to touch the abodes of the four guardians of the horizon and the gods. It consisted of seven precious substances: gold, silver, lapis lazuli, Musaragalva, emerald, red coral, and Karketana-stone. This Stupa of precious substances once formed, the gods of paradise strewed and covered it with Mandarava and great Mandara flowers. And from that Stupa of precious substances there issued this voice: "Excellent, excellent, Lord Sakyamuni! You have well expounded this Dharmaparyaya of the Lotus of the True Dharma. So it is, Bhagavan; so it is, Buddha."

At the sight of that great Stupa of precious substances, that meteoric phenomenon in the sky, the four classes of hearers were filled with gladness delight, satisfaction and joy. Instantly they rose from their seats, stretched out their joined hands, and remained standing in that position. Then the Bodhisattva Mahasattva Mahapratibhana, perceiving the world, including gods, men, and demons, filled with curiosity, said to Bhagavat: "O Bhagavat, what is the cause, what is the reason of so magnificent a Stupa of precious substances appearing in the world? Who is it, O Bhagavat, who causes that sound to go out from the magnificent Stupa of precious substances?"

Thus asked, Bhagavat spoke to Mahapratibhana, the Bodhisattva Mahasattva, as follows: "In this great Stupa of precious substances, Mahapratibhana, the proper body of the Tathagata is contained condensed; his is the Stupa; it is he who causes this sound to go out.

"In the point of space below, Mahapratibhana, there are innumerable thousands of worlds. Further on is the world called Ratnavisuddha, there is the Tathagata named Prabhutaratna, the Arhat. This Tathagata a long time ago made this vow: 'Formerly, when following the course of a Bodhisattva, I have not arrived at supreme, perfect enlightenment before I had heard this Dharmaparyaya of the Lotus of the True Dharma, serving for the instruction of Bodhisattvas. But from the moment that I had heard this Dharmaparyaya of the Lotus of the True Dharma, I have become fully ripe for supreme, perfect enlightenment.' Now Bhagavat Prabhutaratna, the Tathagata, at the juncture of time when his complete extinction was to take place, announced in presence of the world, including the gods: 'After my complete extinction, monks, one Stupa must be made of precious substances of this form of the proper body of the Tathagata; the other Stupas, again, should be made in dedication or in reference to me.' Thereupon, Bhagavat Prabhutaratna, the Tathagata, pronounced this blessing: 'Let my Stupas here, Stupas of my proper bodily form, arise wherever in any Buddha-fields in the ten directions of space, in all worlds, the Dharmaparyaya of the Lotus of the True Dharma is propounded, and let it stand in the sky above the assembled congregation when this Dharmaparyaya of the Lotus of the True Dharma is being preached by some Buddha or another, and let this Stupa of the form of my proper body give a shout of applause to those Buddhas while preaching this Dharmaparyaya of the Lotus of the True Dharma. It is that Stupa of the relics of Bhagavat Prabhutaratna, the Tathagata, which, while I was preaching this Dharmaparyaya of the Lotus of the True Dharma in this Saha-world, arose above this assembled congregation and, standing as a meteor in the sky, gave its applause."

Then said Mahapratibhana, the Bodhisattva Mahasattva, to Bhagavat: "Show us, O Bhagavat, through your power the form of the aforementioned Tathagata."

Whereon Bhagavat spoke to Mahapratibhana as follows: "This Tathagata Prabhutaratna, Mahapratibhana, has made a grave and pious vow. That vow consisted in this: 'When Bhagavats, the Buddhas, being in other Buddha-fields, shall preach this Dharmaparyaya of the Lotus of the True Dharma, then let this Stupa of the form of my proper body be near the Tathagata to hear from him this Dharmaparyaya of the Lotus of the True Dharma. And when those Bhagavats, those Buddhas wish to uncover the form of my proper body and show it to the four classes of hearers, let then the Tathagata-forms, made by the Tathagatas in all quarters, in different Buddha-fields, from their own proper body, and preaching the law to creatures, under different names in several Buddha-fields, let all those Tathagata-forms, made from the proper body, united together, along with this Stupa containing the frame of my own body, be opened and shown to the four classes of hearers.' Therefore, Mahapratibhana, I have made many Tathagata-forms which in all quarters, in several Buddha-fields in thousands of worlds, preach the law to creatures. All those ought to be brought here."

Thereupon the Bodhisattva Mahasattva Mahapratibhana said to Bhagavat: "Then, O Bhagavat, shall we reverentially salute all those bodily emanations of the Tathagata and created by the Tathagata."

And instantly Bhagavat darted from the circle of hair between his brows a ray, which was no sooner darted than Bhagavats, the Buddhas stationed in the east in fifty hundred thousand myriads of kotis of worlds, equal to the sands of the river Ganges, became all visible, and the Buddha-fields there, consisting of crystal, became visible, variegated with jewel trees, decorated with strings of fine cloth, replete with many hundred thousands of Bodhisattvas, covered with canopies, decked with a network of seven precious substances and gold. And in those fields appeared Bhagavats, the Buddhas, teaching with sweet and gentle voice the law to creatures; and those Buddha-fields seemed replete with hundred thousands of Bodhisattvas. So, too, it was in the south-east; so in the south; so in the south-west; so in the west; so in the north-west; so in the north; so in the north-east; so in the nadir; so in the zenith; so in the ten directions of space; in each direction were to be seen many hundred thousand myriads of kotis of Buddha-fields, similar to the sands of the river Ganges, in many worlds similar to the sands of the river Ganges, the Buddhas in many hundred thousand myriads of kotis of Buddha-fields.

Those Tathagatas, in the ten directions of space then addressed each his own troop of Bodhisattvas: "We shall have to go, young men of good family, to the Saha-world near Bhagavat Sakyamuni, the Tathagata, to humbly salute the Stupa of the relics of Prabhutaratna, the Tathagata."

Thereupon those Buddhas resorted with their own satellites, each with one or two, to this Saha-world. At that period this all-embracing world was adorned with jewel trees; it consisted of lapis lazuli, was covered with a network of seven precious substances and gold, smoking with the odorous incense of magnificent jewels, everywhere strewn with Mandarava and great Mandarava flowers, decorated with a network of little bells, showing a checker board divided by gold threads into eight compartments, devoid of villages, towns, boroughs, provinces, kingdoms, and royal capitals, without Kala-mountain, without the mountains Mukilinda and great Mukilinda, without a mount Sumeru, without a Kakravala (horizon) and great Kakravala (extended horizon), without other principal mountains, without great oceans, without rivers and great rivers, without bodies of gods, men, and demons, without hells, without brute creation, without a kingdom of Yama. For it must be understood that at that period all beings in any of the six states of existence in this world had been removed to other worlds, with the exception of those who were assembled at that congregation. Then it was that those Buddhas, attended by one or two satellites, arrived at this Saha-world and went one after the other to occupy their place close to the foot of a jewel tree. Each of the jewel trees was five hundred yoganas in height, had boughs, leaves, foliage, and circumference in proportion, and was provided with blossoms and fruits. At the foot of each jewel tree stood prepared a throne, five yoganas in height, and adorned with magnificent jewels. Each Tathagata went to occupy his throne and sat on it cross-legged. And so all the Tathagatas of the whole sphere sat cross-legged at the foot of the jewel trees.

At that moment the whole sphere was replete with Tathagatas, but the beings produced from the proper body of Bhagavat Sakyamuni had not yet arrived, not even from a single point of the horizon. Then Bhagavat Sakyamuni, the Tathagata, proceeded to make room for those Tathagata-forms that were arriving one after the other. On every side in the eight directions of space appeared twenty hundred thousand myriads of kotis of Buddha-fields of lapis lazuli, decked with a network of seven precious substances and gold, decorated with a fringe of little bells, strewn with

Mandarava and great Mandarava flowers, covered with heavenly awnings, hung with wreaths of heavenly flowers, smoking with heavenly odorous incense. All those twenty hundred thousand myriads of kotis of Buddha-fields were without villages, towns, boroughs, without Kala-mountain, without great oceans, without bodies of gods. All those Buddha-fields were so arranged by him as to form one Buddha-fields, one soil, even, lovely, set off with trees of seven precious substances, trees five hundred yoganas in height and circumference, provided with boughs, flowers, and fruits in proportion. At the foot of each tree stood prepared a throne, five yoganas in height and width, consisting of celestial gems, glittering and beautiful. The Tathagatas arriving one after the other occupied the throne near the foot of each tree, and sat cross-legged. In like manner the Tathagata Sakyamuni prepared twenty hundred thousand myriads of kotis of other worlds, in every direction of space, in order to give room to the Tathagatas who were arriving one after the other. Those twenty hundred thousand myriads of kotis of worlds in every direction of space were likewise so made by him as to be without villages, towns. They were without bodies of gods; all those beings had been removed to other worlds. These Buddha-fields also were of lapis lazuli. All those jewel trees measured five hundred yoganas, and near them were thrones, artificially made and measuring five yoganas. Then those Tathagatas sat down cross-legged, each on a throne at the foot of a jewel tree.

At that moment the Tathagatas produced by Bhagavat Sakyamuni, who in the east were preaching the law to creatures in hundred thousands of myriads of kotis of Buddha-fields, similar to the sands of the river Ganges, all arrived from the ten points of space and sat down in the eight quarters. Thereupon thirty kotis of worlds in each direction were occupied by those Tathagatas from all the eight quarters. Then, seated on their thrones, those Tathagatas deputed their satellites into the presence of Bhagavat Sakyamuni, and after giving them bags with jewel flowers enjoined them thus: "Go, young men of good family, to the Gridhraktila mountain, where Bhagavat Sakyamuni, the Tathagata, is; salute him reverentially and ask, in our name, after the state of health, well-being, lustiness, and comfort both of himself and the crowd of Bodhisattvas and disciples. Strew him with this heap of jewels and speak thus: Would Bhagavat Tathagata deign to open this great Stupa of jewels?" It was in this manner that all those Tathagatas deputed their satellites.

And when Bhagavat Sakyamuni, the Tathagata, perceived that his creations, none wanting, had arrived; perceived that they were severally seated on their thrones, and perceived that the satellites of those Tathagatas, were present, he, in consideration of the wish expressed by those Tathagatas, rose from his seat and stood in the sky, as a meteor. And all the four classes of the assembly rose from their seats, stretched out their joined hands, and stood gazing up to the face of Bhagavat. Bhagavat then, with the right fore-finger, unlocked the middle of the great Stupa of jewels, which showed like a meteor, and so severed the two parts. Even as the double doors of a great city gate separate when the bolt is removed, so Bhagavat opened the great Stupa, which showed like a meteor, by unlocking it in the middle with the right fore-finger. The great Stupa of jewels had no sooner been opened than Bhagavat Prabhutaratna, the Tathagata, was seen sitting cross-legged on his throne, with emaciated limbs and faint body, as if absorbed in abstract meditation, and he pronounced these words: "Excellent, excellent, Bhagavat Sakyamuni; you have well expounded this Dharmaparyaya of the Lotus of the True Dharma. I repeat, you have well expounded this Dharmaparyaya of the Lotus of the True Dharma, Lord Sakyamuni, to the four classes of the assembly. I myself have come here to hear the Dharmaparyaya of the Lotus of the True Dharma."

Now the four classes of the assembly, on perceiving Bhagavat Prabhutaratna, the Tathagata, who had been extinct for many hundred thousand myriads of kotis of Eons, speaking in this way, were filled with wonder and amazement. Instantly they covered Bhagavat Prabhataratna, the Tathagata, and Bhagavat Sakyamuni, the Tathagata, with heaps of divine and human flowers. And then Bhagavat Prabhutaratna, the Tathagata, ceded to Bhagavat Sakyamuni, the Tathagata, the half of the seat on that very throne within that same great Stupa of jewels and said: "Let Bhagavat Sakyamuni, the Tathagata, sit down here."

Whereon Bhagavat Sakyamuni, the Tathagata, sat down upon that half-seat together with the other Tathagata, so that both Tathagatas were seen as meteors in the sky, sitting on the throne in the middle of the great Stupa of jewels.

And in the minds of those four classes of the assembly rose this thought: 'We are far off from the two Tathagatas; therefore let us also, through the power of the Tathagata, rise up to the sky.' As Bhagavat apprehended in his mind what was going on in the minds of those four classes of the assembly, he instantly, by magic power, established the four classes as meteors in the sky.

Thereupon Bhagavat Sakyamuni, the Tathagata, addressed the four classes: "Who amongst you, O monks, will endeavour to expound this Dharmaparyaya of the Lotus of the True Dharma in this Saha-world? The fatal term, the time of death, is now at hand; the Tathagata longs for complete extinction, O monks, after entrusting to you this Dharmaparyaya of the Lotus of the True Dharma."

And on that occasion Bhagavat uttered the following stanzas:

1. Here you see, O monks, the great Seer, the extinct Chief, within the Stupa of jewels, who now has come to hear the law. Who would not call up his energy for the law's sake?

2. Albeit completely extinct for many kotis of Eons, he yet now comes to hear the law; for the law's sake he moves towards here; very rare and very precious is a law like this.

3. This Leader practised a vow when he was in a former existence; even

after his complete extinction he wanders through this whole world in all ten points of space.

4. And all these you here see are my proper bodies, by thousands of kotis, like the sands of the Ganges; they have appeared that the law may be fulfilled I and in order to see this extinct Master.

5. After laying out for each his peculiar field, as well as having created all disciples, men and gods, in order to preserve the true law, as long as the reign of the law shall last,

6. I have by magic power cleared many worlds, destined as seats for those Buddhas, and transported all creatures.

7. It has always been my anxious care how this line of the law might be manifested. So you see Buddhas here in immense number staying at the foot of trees like a great multitude of lotuses.

8. Many kotis of bases of trees are brightened by the Leaders sitting on the thrones which are perpetually occupied by them and brightened as darkness is by fire.

9. A delicious fragrance spreads from the Leaders of the world over all quarters, a fragrance by which, when the wind is blowing, all these creatures are intoxicated.

10. Let him who after my extinction shall keep this Dharmaparyaya quickly pronounce his declaration in the presence of Bhagavats of the world.

11. The Seer Prabhutaratna who, though completely extinct, is awake, will hear the lion's roar of him who shall take this resolution.

12. Myself, in the second place, as well as the many Chiefs who have

flocked here by kotis, will hear that resolution from the son of Jina, who is to exert himself to expound this law.

13. And thereby shall I always be honoured as well as Prabheitaratna, the self-born Jina, who perpetually wanders through the quarters and intermediate quarters in order to hear such a law as this.

14. And these other Leaders of the world here present, by whom this soil is so variegated and splendid, to them also will accrue ample and manifold honour from this Sutra being preached.

15. Here on this seat you see me, together with Bhagavat next to me, in the middle of the Stupa; likewise many other Leaders of the world here present, in many hundreds of fields.

16. You, young men of good family, mind, for mercy's sake towards all beings, that it is a very difficult task to which the Chief urges you.

17. One might expound many thousands of Sutras, like to the sands of the Ganges, without much difficulty.

18. One who after grasping the Sumeru in the fist were to hurl it a distance of kotis of fields, would do nothing very difficult.

19. Nor would it be so very difficult if one could shake this whole universe by the thumb to hurl it a distance of kotis of fields.

20. Nor would one who, after taking stand on the limit of the existing world, were to expound the law and thousands of other Sutras, do something so very difficult.

21. But to keep and preach this Sutra in the dreadful period succeeding the extinction of the Chief of the world, that is difficult.

22. To throw down the totality of ether-element after compressing it in one fist, and to leave it behind after having thrown it away, is not difficult.

23. But to copy a Sutra like this in the period after my extinction, that is difficult.

24. To collect the whole earth-element at a nail's end, cast it away, and then walk off to the Brahma-world,

25. Is not difficult, nor would it require a strength surpassing everybody's strength to do this work of difficulty.

26. Something more difficult than that will he do who in the last days after my extinction shall pronounce this Sutra, were it but a single moment.

27. It will not be difficult for him to walk in the midst of the conflagration at the time of the end of the world, even if he carries with him a load of hay.

28. More difficult it will be to keep this Sutra after my extinction and teach it to a single creature.

29. One may keep the eighty-four thousand divisions of the law and expound them, with the instructions and such as they have been set forth, to kotis of living beings;

30. This is not so difficult; nor is it, to train at the present time monks, and confirm my disciples in the five parts of transcendent knowledge.

31. But more difficult is it to keep this Sutra, believe in it, adhere to it, or expound it again and again.

32. Even he who confirms many thousands of kotis of Arhats, blest with

the possession of the six transcendent faculties (abhignas), like sands of the Ganges,

33. Performs something not so difficult by far as the excellent man does who after my extinction shall keep my sublime law.

34. I have often, in thousands of worlds, preached the law, and today also I preach it with the view that Buddha-knowledge may be obtained.

35. This Sutra is declared the principal of all Sutras; he who keeps in his memory this Sutra, keeps the body of the Jina.

36. Speak, O young men of good family, while the Tathagata is still in your presence, who amongst you is to exert himself in later times to keep the Sutra.

37. Not only I myself shall be pleased, but Bhagavats of the world in general, if one would keep for a moment this Sutra so difficult to keep.

38. Such a one shall ever be praised by all Bhagavats of the world, famed as an eminent hero, and quick in arriving at transcendent wisdom.

39. He shall be entrusted with the leadership amongst the sons of the Tathagatas, he who, after having reached the stage of meekness, shall keep this Sutra.

40. He shall be the eye of the world, including gods and men, who shall speak this Sutra after the extinction of the Chief of men.

41. He is to be venerated by all beings, the wise man who in the last times shall preach this Sutra were it but a single moment.

Thereupon Bhagavat addressed the whole company of Bodhisattvas and the world, including gods and demons, and said: "O monks, in times past long ago I have, unwearied and without repose, sought after the Sutra of the Lotus of the True Dharma, during immense, immeasurable Eons; many Eons before I have been a king, during many thousands of Eons. Having once taken the strong resolution to arrive at supreme, perfect enlightenment, my mind did not swerve from its aim. I exerted myself to fulfil the six Perfections (Paramitas), bestowing immense alms: gold, money, gems, pearls, lapis lazuli, conch-shells, stones, coral, gold and silver, emerald, Musaragalva, red pearls; villages, towns, boroughs, provinces, kingdoms, royal capitals; wives, sons, daughters, slaves, male and female; elephants, horses, cars, up to the sacrifice of life and body, of limbs and members, hands, feet, head. And never did the thought of self-complacency rise in me. In those days the life of men lasted long, so that for a time of many hundred thousand years I was exercising the rule of a King of the Law for the sake of duty, not for the sake of enjoyment. After installing in government the eldest prince royal, I went in quest of the best law in the four quarters, and had promulgated with sound of bell the following proclamation: 'He who procures for me the best laws or points out what is useful, to him will I become a servant.' At that time there lived a Seer; he told me: 'Noble king, there is a Sutra, called the Lotus of the True Dharma, which is an exposition of the best law. If you consent to become my servant, I will teach you that law.' And I, glad, content, exulting and ravished at the words I heard from the Seer, became his pupil, and said: 'I will do for you the work of a servant.' And so having agreed upon becoming the servant of the Seer, I performed the duties of a servitor, such as fetching grass, fuel, water, roots, fruit. I held also the office of a doorkeeper. When I had done such kind of work at day-time, I at night kept his feet while he was lying on his couch, and never did I feel fatigue of body or mind. In such occupations I passed a full millennium."

And for the fuller elucidation of this matter Bhagavat on that occasion uttered the following stanzas:

42. I have a remembrance of past ages when I was Dharmika, the King of

the Law, and exercised the royal sway for duty's sake, not for love's sake, in the interest of the best laws.

43. I let go out in all directions this proclamation: I will become a servant to him who shall explain Dharma. At that time there was a far-seeing Sage, a revealer of the Sutra called the True Dharma.

44. He said to me: 'If you wish to know Dharma, become my servant; then I will explain it to you.' As I heard these words I rejoiced and carefully performed such work as a servant ought to do.

45. I never felt any bodily nor mental weariness since I had become a servant for the sake of the true law. I did my best for real truth's sake, not with a view to win honour or enjoy pleasure.

46. That king meanwhile, strenuously and without engaging in other pursuits, roamed in every direction during thousands of kotis of complete Eons without being able to obtain the Sutra called Dharma.

"Now, O monks, what is your opinion? That it was another who at that time, at that juncture was the king? No, you must certainly not hold that view. For it was myself, who at that time, at that juncture was the king. What then, O monks, is your opinion? That it was another who at that time, at that juncture was the Seer? No, you must certainly not hold that view. For it was this Devadatta himself, the monk I, who at that time, at that juncture was the Seer. Indeed, monks, Devadatta was my good friend. By the aid of Devadatta have I accomplished the six perfect virtues (Paramitas). Noble kindness, noble compassion, noble sympathy, noble indifference, the thirty-two signs of a great man, the eighty lesser marks, the gold-coloured tinge, the ten powers, the fourfold absence of hesitation, the four articles of sociability, the eighteen uncommon properties, magical power, ability to save beings in all directions of space - all this have I got after having come to Devadatta. I announce to you, O monks, I declare to you that this

Devadatta, the monk, shall in an age to come, after immense, innumerable Eons, become a Tathagata named Devaraga (King of the gods), an Arhat, in the world Devasopana (Stairs of the gods). The lifetime of that Tathagata Devaraga, O monks, shall measure twenty intermediate kalpas. He shall preach the law in extension, and beings equal to the sands of the river Ganges shall through him forsake all evils and realise Arhatship. Several beings shall also elevate their minds to Pratyekabuddhaship, whereas beings equal to the sands of the river Ganges shall elevate their minds to supreme, perfect enlightenment, and become endowed with unflinching patience. Further, O monks, after the complete extinction of the Tathagata Devaragu, his true law shall stay twenty intermediate kalpas. His body shall not be seen divided into different parts and relics; it shall remain as one mass within a Stupa of seven precious substances, which Stupa is to be sixty hundred yoganas in height and forty yoganas in extension. All, gods and men, shall do worship to it with flowers, incense, perfumed garlands, unguents, powder, clothes, umbrellas, banners, flags, and celebrate it with stanzas and songs. Those who shall turn round that Stupa from left to right or humbly salute it, shall some of them realise Arhatship, others attain Pratyekabuddhaship; others, gods and men, in immense number, shall raise their minds to supreme, perfect enlightenment, never to return."

Thereafter Bhagavat again addressed the assembly of monks: "Whosoever in future, O monks, be he a young man or a young lady of good family, shall hear this chapter of the Sutra of the Lotus of the True Dharma, and by doing so be relieved from doubt, become pure-minded, and put reliance on it, to such a one the door of the three states of misfortune shall be shut. He shall not fall so low as to be born in hell, among beasts, or in Yama's kingdom. When born in the Buddha-fields in the ten points of space he shall at each repeated birth hear this very Sutra, and when born amongst gods or men he shall attain an eminent rank. And in the Buddha-fields where he is to be born he shall appear by metamorphosis on a lotus of seven precious substances, face to face with the Tathagata."

At that moment a Bodhisattva of the name of Pragnakuta, having come from beneath the Buddha-fields of the Tathagatna, said to the Tathagata Prabhutaratna: "O Bhagavat, let us resort to our own Buddha-fields."

But Bhagavat Sakyamuni, the Tathagata, said to the Bodhisattva Pragnakuta: "Wait a while, young man of good family, first have a discussion with my Bodhisattva Mangusri, the prince royal, to settle some point of the law."

And at the same moment, Mangusri, the prince royal, rose seated on a centifolious lotus that was large as a carriage yoked with four horses, surrounded and attended by many Bodhisattvas, from the bosom of the sea, from the abode of the Naga-king Sagara (Ocean). Rising high into the sky he went through the air to the Gridhrakuta mountain to the presence of Bhagavat. There Mangusri, the prince royal, alighted from his lotus, reverentially saluted the feet of Bhagavat Sakyamuni and Prabhutaratna, the Tathagata, went up to the Bodhisattva Pragnakuta and, after making the usual complimentary questions as to his health and welfare, seated himself at some distance. The Bodhisattva Pragnakuta then addressed to Mangusri, the prince royal, the following question: "Mangusri, how many beings have you educated during your stay in the sea?"

Mangusri answered: "Many, innumerable, incalculable beings have I educated, so innumerable that words cannot express it, nor thought conceive it. Wait a while, young man of good family, you shall presently see a token."

No sooner had Mangusri, the prince royal, spoken these words than instantaneously many thousands of lotuses rose from the bosom of the sea up to the sky, and on those lotuses were seated many thousands of Bodhisattvas, who flocked through the air to the Gridhrakilla, mountain, where they stayed, appearing as meteors. All of them had been educated by Mangusri, the prince royal, to supreme, perfect enlightenment. The Bodhisattvas amongst them who had formerly striven after the great vehicle extolled the virtues of the great vehicle and the six perfect virtues (Paramitas). Such as had been disciples extolled the vehicle of disciples. But all acknowledged the voidness of all phenomena (or things), as well as the virtues of the great vehicle. Mangusri, the prince royal, said to the Bodhisattva Pragntakuta: "Young man of good family, while I was staying in the bosom of the great ocean I have by all means educated creatures, and here you saw the result."

Whereupon the Bodhisattva Pragnakuta questioned Mangusri, the prince royal, in chanting the following stanzas:

47. O you, Blessed one, who from your wisdom are called the Sage, by whose power is it that you now have educated those innumerable beings? Tell it me upon my question:

48. 'What law have you preached, or what Sutra, in showing the path of enlightenment, so that those who are there with you have conceived the idea of enlightenment? That, once having gained a safe ford, they have been decisively established in omniscience?'

Mangusri answered: "In the bosom of the sea I have expounded the Lotus of the True Dharma and no other Sutra."

Pragnakuta said: "That Sutra is profound, subtle, difficult to seize; no other Sutra equals it. Is there any creature able to understand this jewel of a Sutra or to arrive at supreme, perfect enlightenment?"

Mangusri replied: "There is, young man of good family, the daughter of Sagara, the Naga-king, eight years old, very intelligent, of keen faculties, endowed with prudence in acts of body, speech, and mind, who has caught and kept all the teachings, in substance and form, of the Tathagatas, who has acquired in one moment a thousand meditations and proofs of the essence of all laws. She does not swerve from the idea of enlightenment, has great aspirations, applies to other beings the same measure as to herself; she is apt to display all virtues and is never deficient in them. With a bland smile on

179

the face and in the bloom of an extremely handsome appearance she speaks words of kindliness and compassion. She is fit to arrive at supreme, perfect enlightenment."

The Bodhisattva Praggakuta said: "I have seen how Bhagavat Sakyamuni, the Tathagata, when he was striving after enlightenment, in the state of a Bodhisattva, performed innumerable good works and during many Eons never slackened in his arduous task. In the whole universe there is not a single spot so small as a mustard-seed where he has not surrendered his body for the sake of creatures. Afterwards he arrived at enlightenment. Who then would believe that she should have been able to arrive at supreme, perfect knowledge in one moment?"

At that very moment appeared the daughter of Sagara, the Naga-king, standing before their face. After reverentially saluting the feet of Bhagavat she stationed herself at some distance and uttered on that occasion the following stanzas:

49. Spotless, bright, and of unfathomable light is that ethereal body, adorned with the thirty-two characteristic signs, pervading space in all directions.

50. He is possessed of the secondary marks and praised by every being, and accessible to all, like an open market-place.

51. I have obtained enlightenment according to my wish; the Tathagata can bear witness to it; I will extensively reveal the law that releases from sufferance.

Then the venerable Sariputra said to that daughter of Sagara, the Naga-king: "You have conceived the idea of enlightenment, young lady of good family, without sliding back, andaregifted with immense wisdom, but supreme, perfect enlightenment is not easily won. It may happen, sister, that a woman displays an unflagging energy, performs good works for many thousands of Eons, and fulfils the six perfect virtues (Paramitas), but as yet there is no example of her having reached Buddhaship, and that because a woman cannot occupy the five ranks: the rank of Brahma; the rank of Indra; the rank of a chief guardian of the four quarters; the rank of Kakravartin; the rank of a Bodhisattva incapable of sliding back."

Now the daughter of Sagara, the Naga-king, had at the time a gem which in value outweighed the whole universe. That gem the daughter of Sagara, the Naga-king, presented to Bhagavat, and Bhagavat graciously accepted it. Then the daughter of Sagara, the Naga-king, said to the Bodhisattva Pragnakuta and the senior priest Sariputra: "Has Bhagavat readily accepted the gem I presented him or has he not?"

Then the venerable Sariputra answered: "As soon as it was presented by you, so soon it was accepted by Bhagavat."

The daughter of Sagara, the Naga-king, replied: "If I were endowed with magic power, brother Sariputra, I should sooner have arrived at supreme, perfect enlightenment, and there would have been none to receive this gem."

At the same instant, before the sight of the whole world and of the venerable Sariputra, the female daughter of Sagara, the Naga-king, disappeared; the male appeared as she manifested herself as a Bodhisattva, who immediately went to the South to sit down at the foot of a tree made of seven precious substances, in the world Vimala (Spotless), where he showed himself enlightened and preaching the law, while filling all directions of space with the radiance of the thirty-two characteristic signs and all secondary marks. All beings in the Saha-world beheld that Lord while he received the homage of all, gods, Nagas, goblins, Gandharvas, demons, Garudas, Kinnaras, great serpents, men, and beings not human, and was engaged in preaching the law. And the beings who heard the preaching of that Tathagata became incapable of sliding back in supreme, perfect enlightenment. And that world Vimala and this Saha-world shook in six different ways. Three thousand living beings from the congregational circle of Bhagavat Sakyamuni gained the acquiescence in the eternal law, whereas three hundred thousand beings obtained the prediction of their future destiny to supreme, perfect enlightenment.

Then the Bodhisattva Pragnakuta and the venerable Sariputra were silent.

PART XII.

EXERTION

Thereafter the Bodhisattva Bhaishagyaraga and the Bodhisattva Mahapratibhana, with a retinue of twenty hundred thousand Bodhisattvas, spoke before the face of Bhagavat the following words: "Let Bhagavat be at ease in this respect; we will after the extinction of the Tathagata expound this Paryaya to all creatures, though we are aware, O Bhagavat, that at that period there shall be malign beings, having few roots of goodness, conceited, fond of gain and honour, rooted in unholiness, difficult to tame, deprived of good will, and full of unwillingness. Nevertheless, O Bhagavat, we will at that period read, keep, preach, write, honour, respect, venerate, worship this Sutra. With sacrifice of body and life, O Bhagavat, we will divulge this Sutra. Let Bhagavat be at ease."

Thereupon five hundred monks of the assembly, both such as were under training and such as were not, said to Bhagavat: "We also, O Bhagavat, will exert ourselves to divulge this Dharmaparyaya, though in other worlds."

Then all the disciples of Bhagavat, both such as were under training and such as were not, who had received from Bhagavat the prediction as to their future supreme enlightenment, all the eight thousand monks raised their joined hands towards Bhagavat and said: "Let Bhagavat be at ease. We also will divulge this Dharmaparyaya, after the complete extinction of Bhagavat, in the last days, the last period, though in other worlds. For in this Saha-world, O Bhagavat, the creatures are conceited, possessed of few roots of goodness, always vicious in their thoughts, wicked, and naturally perverse."

Then the noble matron Gautami, the sister of Bhagavat's mother, along with six hundred nuns, some of them being under training, some being not, rose from her seat, raised the joined hands towards Bhagavat and remained gazing up to him. Then Bhagavat addressed the noble matron Gautami: "Why do you stand so dejected, gazing up to the Tathagata?"

She replied: "I have not been mentioned by the Tathagata, nor have I received from him a prediction of my destiny to supreme, perfect enlightenment."

He said: "But, Gautami, you have received a prediction with the prediction regarding the whole assembly. Indeed, Gautami, you shall from henceforward, before the face of thirty-eight hundred thousand myriads of kotis of Buddhas, be a Bodhisattva and preacher of the law. These six thousand nuns also, partly perfected in discipline, partly not, shall along with others become Bodhisattvas and preachers of the law before the face of the Tathagatas. Afterwards, when you shall have completed the course of a Bodhisattva, you shall become, under the name of Sarvasattvapriyadarsana (Lovely to see for all beings), a Tathagata, an Arhat, endowed with science and conduct. And that Tathagata Sarvasattvapriyadarsana, O Gautami, shall give a prediction by regular succession to those six thousand Bodhisattvas concerning their destiny to supreme, perfect enlightenment."

Then the nun Yasodhara, the mother of Rahula, thought thus: 'Bhagavat has not mentioned my name.'

And Bhagavat comprehending in his own mind what was going on in the mind of the nun Yasodhara said to her: "I announce to you, Yasodhara, I declare to you: you also shall before the face of ten thousand kotis of Buddhas become a Bodhisattva and preacher of the law, and after regularly completing the course of a Bodhisattva you shall become a Tathagata, named Rasmisatasahasraparipurnadhvaga, an Arhat, endowed with science and conduct, in the world Bhadra; and the lifetime of that Leader Rasmisatasahasrapariptirnadhvaga shall be unlimited."

When the noble matron Gautami, the nun, with her suite of six thousand nuns, and Yasodhara, the nun, with her suite of four thousand nuns, heard from Bhagavat their future destiny to supreme, perfect enlightenment, they uttered, in wonder and amazement, this stanza:

1. O Bhagavat, you are the trainer, you are the leader; you are the master of the world, including the gods; you are the giver of comfort, you who are worshipped by men and gods. Now, indeed, we feel satisfied."

After uttering this stanza the nuns said to Bhagavat: "We also, O Bhagavat, will exert ourselves to divulge this Dharmaparyaya in the last days, though in other worlds."

Thereafter Bhagavat looked towards the eighty hundred thousand Bodhisattvas who were gifted with magical spells and capable of moving forward the wheel that never rolls back. No sooner were those Bodhisattvas regarded by Bhagavat than they rose from their seats, raised their joined hands towards Bhagavat and reflected thus: "Bhagavat invites us to make known the Dharmaparyaya."

Agitated by that thought they asked one another: "What shall we do, young men of good family, in order that this Dharmaparyaya may in future be made known as Bhagavat invites us to do?"

Thereupon those young men of good family, in consequence of their reverence for Bhagavat and their own pious vow in their previous course, raised a lion's roar before Bhagavat: "We, O Bhagavat, will in future, after the complete extinction of Bhagavat, go in all directions in order that creatures shall write, keep, meditate, divulge this Dharmaparyaya, by no other's power but Bhagavat's. And Bhagavat, staying in another world, shall protect, defend, and guard us."

Then the Bodhisattvas unanimously in a chorus addressed Bhagavat with the following stanzas:

2. Be at ease, O Bhagavat. After your complete extinction, in the horrible last period of the world, we will proclaim this sublime Sutra.

3. We will suffer, patiently endure, O Bhagavat, the injuries, threats, blows and threats with sticks at the hands of foolish men.

4. At that dreadful last epoch men will be malign, crooked, wicked, dull, conceited, fancying to have come to the limit when they have not.

5. We do not care but to live in the wilderness and wear a patched cloth; we lead a frugal life;" so will they speak to the ignorant.

6. And persons greedily attached to enjoyments will preach the law to laymen and be honoured as if they possessed the six transcendent qualities.

7. Cruel-minded and wicked men, only occupied with household cares, will enter our retreat in the forest and become our calumniators.

8. The Tirthikas, themselves bent on profit and honour, will say of us that we are so, and -shame on such monks!-they will preach their own fictions.

9. Prompted by greed of profit and honour they will compose Sutras of their own invention and then, in the midst of the assembly, accuse us of plagiarism.

10. To kings, princes, king's peers, as well as to Brahmans and commoners,

and to monks of other confessions,

11. They will speak evil of us and propagate the Tirtha-doctrine. We will endure all that out of reverence for the great Seers.

12. And those fools who will not listen to us, shall sooner or later become enlightened, and therefore will we forbear to the last.

13. In that dreadful, most terrible period of frightful general revolution will many fiendish monks stand up as our revilers.

14. Out of respect for the Chief of the world we will bear it, however difficult it be; girded with the girdle of forbearance will I proclaim this Sutra.

15. I do not care for my body or life, O Bhagavat, but as keepers of thine entrusted deposit we care for enlightenment.

16. Bhagavat himself knows that in the last period there are to be wicked monks who do not understand mysterious speech.

17. One will have to bear frowning looks, repeated disavowal, expulsion from the monasteries, many and manifold abuses.

18. Yet mindful of the command of Bhagavat of the world we will in the last period undauntedly proclaim this Sutra in the midst of the congregation.

19. We will visit towns and villages everywhere, and transmit to those who care for it thine entrusted deposit, O Bhagavat.

20. O Chief of the world, we will deliver your message; be at ease then, great Seer.

21. Light of the world, you know the disposition of all who have flocked

here from every direction, and you know that we speak a word of truth.

PART XIII.

PEACEFUL LIFE

Mangusri, the prince royal, said to Bhagavat: "It is difficult, O Bhagavat, most difficult, what these Bodhisattvas Mahasattvas will attempt out of reverence for Bhagavat. How are these Bodhisattvas Mahasattvas to promulgate this Dharmaparyaya at the end of time, at the last period?"

Whereupon Bhagavat answered Mangusri, the prince royal: "A Bodhisattva Mahasattva, Mangusri, he who is to promulgate this Dharmaparyaya at the end of time, at the last period, must be firm in four things. In which things? The Bodhisattva Mahasattva, Mangusri, must be firm in his conduct and proper sphere if he wishes to teach this Dharmaparyaya. And how, Mangusri, is a Bodhisattva Mahasattva firm in his conduct and proper sphere? When the Bodhisattva Mahasattva, Mangusri, is patient, meek, has reached the stage of meekness; when he is not rash, nor envious; when, moreover, Mangusri, he clings to no law whatever and sees the real character of the phenomena; when he is refraining from investigating and discussing these laws, Mangusri; that is called the conduct of a Bodhisattva Mahasattva. And what is the proper sphere of a Bodhisattva Mahasattva, Mangusri? When the Bodhisattva Mahasattva, Mangusri, does not serve, not court, not wait upon kings; does not serve, not court, not wait upon princes; when he does not approach them; when he does not serve, not court, not wait upon persons of another sect, Karakas, Parivragakas, Agivakas, Nirgranthas, nor persons passionately fond of fine literature; when he does not serve, not court, not wait upon adepts at worldly spells, and votaries of a worldly philosophy, nor keep any communication with them; when he does not go to see Kandalas, jugglers, vendors of pork, poulterers, deer-hunters, butchers, actors and dancers, wrestlers, nor resort to places where others flock for amusement and sport; when he keeps no communication with them unless from time to time to preach the law to them when they come to him, and that freely; when he does not serve, not court, not wait upon monks, nuns, lay devotees, male and female, who are adherents of the vehicle of disciples, nor keep communication with them; when he does not come in contact with them at the place of promenade or in the monastery, unless from time to time to preach the law to them when they come to him, and even that freely. This, Mangusri, is the proper sphere of a Bodhisattva Mahasattva.

"Again, Mangusri, the Bodhisattva Mahasattva does not take hold of some favourable opportunity or another to preach the law to females every now and anon, nor is he desirous of repeatedly seeing females; nor does he think it proper to visit families and then too often address a girl, virgin, or young wife, nor does he greet them too fondly in return. He does not preach the law to a hermaphrodite, keeps no communication with such a person, nor greets too friendly in return. He does not enter a house alone in order to receive alms, unless having the Tathagata in his thoughts. And when he happens to preach the law to females, he does not do so by passionate attachment to the law, far less by passionate attachment to a woman. When he is preaching, he does not display his row of teeth, let alone a quick emotion on his physiognomy. He addresses no novice, male or female, no nun, no monk, no young boy, no young girl, nor enters upon a conversation with them; he shows no great readiness in answering their address, nor cares to give too frequent answers. This, Mangusri, is called the first proper sphere of a Bodhisattva Mahasattva.

"Further, Mangusri, a Bodhisattva Mahasattva looks upon all phenomena (things) as void; he sees them duly established, remaining unaltered, as they are in reality, not liable to be disturbed, not to be moved backward, unchangeable, existing in the absolute sense of the word, having the nature of space, escaping explanation and expression by means of common speech, not born, composed and simple, aggregated and isolated, not expressible in words, independently established, manifesting themselves owing to a perversion of perception. In this way then, Mangusri, the Bodhisattva Mahasattva constantly views all laws, and if he abides in this course, he remains in his own sphere. This, Mangusri, is the second proper sphere of a Bodhisattva Mahasattva."

And in order to expound this matter in greater detail, Bhagavat uttered the following stanzas :

1. The Bodhisattva who, undaunted and unabashed, wishes to set forth this Sutra in the dreadful period hereafter,

2. Must keep to his course of duty and proper sphere; he must be retired and pure, constantly avoid communication with kings and princes.

3. Nor should he keep up communication with king's servants, nor with Kandalas, jugglers, and Tirthikas in general.

4. He ought not to court conceited men, but catechise such as keep to the religion. He must also avoid such monks as follow the precepts of the Arhat (of the Gainas), and immoral men.

5. He must be constant in avoiding a nun who is fond of banter and chatter; he must also avoid notoriously loose female lay devotees.

6. He should shun any communication with such female lay devotees as seek their highest happiness in this transient world. This is called the proper conduct of a Bodhisattva.

7. But when one comes to him to question him about the law for the sake of superior enlightenment, he should, at any time, speak freely, always firm and undaunted.

8. He should have no communication with women and hermaphrodites; he

should also shun the young wives and girls in families.

9. He must never address them to ask after their health. He must also avoid communication with vendors of pork and mutton.

10. With any persons who slay animals of various kind for the sake of profit, and with such as sell meat he should avoid having any communication.

11. He must shun the society of whoremongers, players, musicians, wrestlers, and other people of that sort.

12. He should not frequent whores, nor other sensual persons; he must avoid any exchange of civility with them.

13. And when the sage has to preach for a woman, he should not enter into an apartment with her alone, nor stay to banter.

14. When he has often to enter a village in quest of food, he must have another monk with him or constantly think of the Buddha.

15. Herewith have I shown the first sphere of proper conduct. Wise are they who, keeping this Sutra in memory, live according to it.

16. And when one observes no law at all, low, superior or mean, composed or uncomposed, real or not real;

17. When the wise man does not remark, 'This is a woman,' nor marks, 'This is a man;' when in searching he finds no phenomena, because they have never existed;

18. This is called the observance of the Bodhisattvas in general. Now listen to me when I set forth what should be their proper sphere.

19. All phenomena (things) have been declared to be non-existing, not appearing, not produced, void, immovable, everlasting; this is called the proper sphere of the wise.

20. They have been divided into existing and non-existing, real and unreal, by those who had wrong notions; other laws also, of permanency, of being produced, of birth from something already produced, are wrongly assumed.

21. Let the Bodhisattva be concentrated in mind, attentive, ever firm as the peak of Mount Sumeru, and in such a state of mind look upon all phenomena (things) as having the nature of space, being void.

22. Permanently equal to space, without essence, immovable, without substantiality. These, indeed, are the laws, all and forever. This is called the proper sphere of the wise.

23. The monk observing this rule of conduct given by me may, after my extinction, promulgate this Sutra in the world, and shall feel no depression.

24. Let the sage first, for some time, coerce his thoughts, exercise meditation with complete absorption, and correctly perform all that is required for attaining spiritual insight, and then, after rising from his pious meditation, preach with unquailing mind.

25. The kings of this earth and the princes who listen to the law protect him. Others also, both laymen and Brahmans, will be found together in his congregation.

"Further, Mangusri, the Bodhisattva Mahasattva who, after the complete extinction of the Tathagata at the end of time, the last period, the last five hundred years, when the true law is in a state of decay, is going to propound this Dharmaparyaya, must be in a peaceful state of mind and then preach the law, whether he knows it by heart or has it in a book. In his sermon he will not be too prone to carping at others, not blame other preaching friars, not speak scandal nor propagate scandal. He does not mention by name other monks, adherents of the vehicle of disciples, to propagate scandal. He cherishes even no hostile feelings against them, because he is in a peaceful state. All who come, one after the other, to hear the sermon he receives with benevolence, and preaches the law to them without invidiousness. He refrains from entering upon a dispute; but if he is asked a question, he does not answer in the way of those who follow the vehicle of disciples; on the contrary, he answers as if he had attained Buddha-knowledge."

And on that occasion Bhagavat uttered the following stanzas :

26. The wise man is always at ease, and in that state he preaches the law, seated on an elevated pulpit which has been prepared for him on a clean and pretty spot.

27. He puts on a clean, nice, red robe, dyed with good colours, and a black woollen garment and a long undergarment,

28. Having duly washed his feet and rubbed his head and face with smooth ointments, he ascends the pulpit, which is provided with a footbank and covered with pieces of fine cloth of various sorts, and sits down.

29. When he is thus seated on the preacher's pulpit and all who have gathered round him are attentive, he proceeds to deliver many discourses, pleasing by variety, before monks and nuns,

30. Before male and female lay devotees, kings and princes. The wise man always takes care to deliver a sermon diversified in its contents and sweet, free from invidiousness.

31. If occasionally he is asked some question, even after he has commenced, he will explain the matter anew in regular order, and he will explain it in

such away that his hearers gain enlightenment.

32. The wise man is indefatigable; not even the thought of fatigue will rise in him; he knows no listlessness, and so displays to the assembly the strength of charity.

33. Day and night the wise man preaches this sublime law with myriads of kotis of illustrations; he edifies and satisfies his audience without ever requiring anything.

34. Solid food, soft food, nourishment and drink, cloth, couches, robes, medicaments for the sick, all this does not occupy his thoughts, nor does he want anything from the congregation.

35. On the contrary, the wise man is always thinking: 'How can I and these beings become Buddhas? I will preach this true law, upon which the happiness of all beings depends, for the benefit of the world.'

36. The monk who, after my extinction, shall preach in this way, without envy, shall not meet with trouble, impediment, grief or despondency.

37. Nobody shall frighten him, beat or blame him; never shall he be driven away, because he is firm in the strength of forbearance.

38. The wise man who is peaceful, so disposed as I have just said, possesses hundreds of kotis of advantages, so many that one would not be able to enumerate them in hundreds of Eons.

"Again, Mangusri, the Bodhisattva Mahasattva who lives after the extinction of the Tathagata at the end of time when the true law is in decay, the Bodhisattva Mahasattva who keeps this Sutra is not envious, not false, not deceitful; he does not speak disparagingly of other adherents of the vehicle of Bodhisattvas, nor defame, nor humble them. He does not bring forward the shortcomings of other monks, nuns, male and female lay devotees, neither of the adherents of the vehicle of disciples nor of those of the vehicle of Pratyekabuddhas. He does not say: 'You, young men of good family, you are far off from supreme, perfect enlightenment; you give proof of not having arrived at it; you are too fickle in your doings and not capable of acquiring true knowledge.' He does not in this way bring forward the shortcomings of any adherent of the vehicle of the Bodhisattvas. Nor does he show any delight in disputes about the law, or engage in disputes about the law, and he never abandons the strength of charity towards all beings. In respect to all Tathagatas he feels as if they were his fathers, and in respect to all Bodhisattvas as if they were his masters. And as to the Bodhisattvas Mahasattvas in all directions of space, he is assiduous in paying homage to them by good will and respect. When he preaches the law, he preaches no less and no more than the law, without partial predilection for any part of the law, and he does not show greater favour to one than to another, even from love of the law.

"Such, Mangusri, is the third quality with which a Bodhisattva Mahasattva is endowed who is to expound this Dharmaparyaya after the extinction of the Tathagata at the end of time when the true law is in decay; who will live at ease and not be annoyed in the exposition of this Dharmaparyaya. And in the synod he will have allies, and he will find auditors at his sermons who will listen to this Dharmaparyaya, believe, accept, keep, read, penetrate, write it and cause it to be written, and who, after it has been written and a volume made of it, will honour, respect, esteem, and worship it."

This said Bhagavat, and thereafter he, the Buddha, the Master, added the following:

39. The wise man, the preacher, who wishes to expound this Sutra must absolutely renounce falsehood, pride, calumny, and envy.

40. He should never speak a disparaging word of anybody; never engage in

a dispute on religious belief; never say to such as are guilty of shortcomings: 'You will not obtain superior knowledge.'

41. He is always sincere, mild, forbearing; as a true son of Buddha he will repeatedly preach the law without any feeling of vexation.

42. The wise man respects the Bodhisattvas as his masters, thus thinking: 'The Bodhisattvas in all directions of space, who out of compassion for creatures are moving in the world, are my teachers.'

43. Cherishing the memory of the Buddhas, the supreme amongst men, he will always feel towards them as if they were his fathers, and by forsaking all idea of pride he will escape hindrance.

44. The wise man who has heard this law, should be constant in observing it. If he earnestly strives after a peaceful life, kotis of beings will surely protect him.

"Further, Mangusri, the Bodhisattva Mahasattva, living at the time of destruction of the true law after the extinction of the Tathagata, who is desirous of keeping this Dharmaparyaya, should live as far as possible away from laymen and friars, and lead a life of charity. He must feel affection for all beings who are striving for enlightenment and therefore make this reflection: 'To be sure, they are greatly perverted in mind, those beings who do not hear, nor perceive, nor understand the skilfulness and the mystery of the Tathagata, who do not inquire for it, nor believe in it, nor even are willing to believe in it. Of course, these beings do not penetrate, nor understand this Dharmaparyaya. Nevertheless will I, who have attained this supreme, perfect knowledge, powerfully bend to it the mind of every one, whatever may be the position he occupies, and bring about that he accepts, understands, and arrives at full ripeness.'

"By possessing also this fourth quality, Mangusri, a Bodhisattva Mahasattva, who is to expound the law after the extinction of the Tathagata, will be unmolested, honoured, respected, esteemed, venerated by monks, nuns, and lay devotees, male and female, by kings, princes, ministers, king's officers, by citizens and country people, by Brahmans and laymen; the gods of the sky will, full of faith, follow his track to hear the law, and the angels will follow his track to protect him; whether he is in a village or in a monastery, they will approach him day and night to put questions about the law, and they will be satisfied, charmed with his explanation. For this Dharmaparyaya, Mangusri, has been blessed by all Buddhas. With the past, future, and present Tathagata, Mangusri, this Dharmaparyaya is for ever blessed. Precious in all worlds, Mangusri, is the sound, rumour, or mentioning of this Dharmaparyaya.

"It is a case, Mangusri, similar to that of a king, a ruler of armies, who by force has conquered his own kingdom, whereupon other kings, his adversaries, wage war against him. That ruler of armies has soldiers of various description to fight with various enemies. As the king sees those soldiers fighting, he is delighted with their gallantry, enraptured, and in his delight and rapture he makes to his soldiers several donations, such as villages and village grounds, towns and grounds of a town; garments and head-gear; hand-ornaments, necklaces, gold threads, earrings, strings of pearls, bullion, gold, gems, pearls, lapis lazuli, conch-shells, stones, corals; he gives elephants, horses, cars, foot soldiers, servants, vehicles, and litters. But to none he makes a present of his crown jewel, because that jewel only fits on the head of a king. Were the king to give away that crown jewel, then that whole royal army, consisting of four divisions, would be astonished and amazed. In the same manner, Mangusri, the Tathagata, the Arhat, exercises the reign of righteousness and of the law in the triple world which he has conquered by the power of his arm and the power of his virtue. His triple world is assailed by Mara, the Evil One. Then the Aryas, the soldiers of the Tathagata, fight with Mara. Then, Mangusri, the king of the law, Bhagavat of the law, expounds to the Aryas, his soldiers, whom he sees fighting, hundred thousands of Sutras in order to encourage the four classes. He gives them the city of Nirvana, the great city of the law; he allures them with that city of Nirvana, but he does not preach to them such a Dharmaparyaya as this. Just as in that case, Mangusri, that king, ruler of armies, astonished at the great valour of his soldiers in battle gives them all his property, at last even his crown jewel, and just as that crown jewel has been kept by the king on his head to the last, so, Mangusri, the Tathagata, the Arhat, who as the great king of the law in the triple world exercises his sway with justice, when he sees disciples and Bodhisattvas fighting against the Mara of fancies or the Mara of sinful inclinations, and when he sees that by fighting they have destroyed affection, hatred, and infatuation, overcome the triple world and conquered all Maras, is satisfied, and in his satisfaction he expounds to those noble soldiers this Dharmaparyaya which meets opposition in all the world, the unbelief of all the world, a Dharmaparyaya never before preached, never before explained. And the Tathagata bestows on all disciples the noble crown jewel, that most exalted crown jewel which brings omniscience to all. For this, Mangusri, is the supreme preaching of the Tathagatas; this is the last Dharmaparyaya of the Tathagatas; this is the most profound discourse on the law, a Dharmaparyaya meeting opposition in all the world. In the same manner, Mangusri, as that king of righteousness and ruler of armies took off the crown jewel which he had kept so long a time and gave it at last to the soldiers, so, Mangusri, the Tathagata now reveals this long-kept mystery of the law exceeding all others, the mystery which must be known by the Tathagatas."

And in order to elucidate this matter more in detail, Bhagavat on that occasion uttered the following stanzas:

45. Always displaying the strength of charity, always filled with compassion for all creatures, expounding this law, the Buddhas have approved this exalted Sutra.

46. The laymen, as well as the mendicant friars, and the Bodhisattvas who shall live at the end of time, must all show the strength of charity, lest those who hear the law reject it.

47. But I, when I shall have reached enlightenment and be established in Tathagataship, will initiate others, and after having initiated disciples preach everywhere this superior enlightenment.

48. It is a case like that of a king, ruler of armies, who gives to his soldiers various things, gold, elephants, horses, cars, foot soldiers; he also gives towns and villages, in token of his contentment.

49. In his satisfaction he gives to some hand-ornaments, silver and gold thread; pearls, gems, conch-shells, stones, coral; he also gives slaves of various description.

50. But when he is struck with the incomparable daring of one amongst the soldiers, he says: 'You have admirably done this!' and, taking off his crown, makes him a present of the jewel.

51. Likewise do I, the Buddha, the king of the law, I who have the force of patience and a large treasure of wisdom, with justice govern the whole world, benign, compassionate, and pitiful.

52. And seeing how the creatures are in trouble, I pronounce thousands of kotis of Sutrantas, when I perceive the heroism of those living beings who by pure-mindedness overcome the sinful inclinations of the world.

53. And the king of the law, the great physician, who expounds hundreds of kotis of Paryayas, when he recognises that creatures are strong, shows them this Sutra, comparable to a crown jewel.

54. This is the last Sutra proclaimed in the world, the most eminent of all my Sutras, which I have always kept and never divulged. Now I am going to make it known; listen all.

55. There are four qualities to be acquired by those who at the period after my extinction desire supreme enlightenment and perform my charge. The qualities are such as follows:

56. The wise man knows no vexation, trouble, sickness; the colour of his skin is not blackish; nor does he dwell in a miserable town.

57. The great Sage has always a pleasant look, deserves to be honoured, as if he were the Tathagata himself, and little angels shall constantly be his attendants.

58. His body can never be hurt by weapons, poison, sticks, or clods, and the mouth of the man who utters a word of abuse against him shall be closed.

59. He is a friend to all creatures in the world. He goes all over the earth as a light, dissipating the gloom of many kotis of creatures, he who keeps this Sutra after my extinction.

60. In his sleep he sees visions in the shape of Buddha; he sees monks and nuns appearing on thrones and proclaiming the many-sided law.

61. He sees in his dream gods and goblins, numerous as the sands of the Ganges, as well as demons and Nagas of many kinds, who lift their joined hands and to whom he expounds the eminent law.

62. He sees in his dream the Tathagata preaching the law to many kotis of beings with lovely voice, Bhagavat with golden colour.

63. And he stands there with joined hands glorifying the Seer, the highest of men, whilst the Jina, the great physician, is expounding the law to the four classes.

64. And he, glad to have heard the law, joyfully pays his worship, and

after having soon reached the knowledge which never slides back, he obtains, in dream, magical spells.

65. And Bhagavat of the world, perceiving his good intention, announces to him his destiny of becoming a leader amongst men: 'Young man of good family, you shall here reach in future supreme, holy knowledge.

66. 'You shall have a large field and four classes of hearers, even as myself, that respectfully and with joined hands shall hear from you the vast and faultless law.'

67. Again he sees his own person occupied with meditating on the law in mountain caverns; and by meditating he attains the very nature of the law and, on obtaining complete absorption, sees the Jina.

68. And after seeing in his dream the gold coloured one, him who displays a hundred hallowed signs, he hears the law, whereafter he preaches it in the assembly. Such is his dream.

69. And in his dream he also forsakes his whole realm, harem, and numerous kinsfolk; renouncing all pleasures he leaves home to become an ascetic, and betakes himself to the place of the terrace of enlightenment.

70. There, seated upon a throne at the foot of a tree to seek enlightenment, he will, after the lapse of seven days, arrive at the knowledge of the Tathagatas.

71. On having reached enlightenment he will rise up from that place to move forward the faultless wheel and preach the law during an inconceivable number of thousands of kotis of Eons.

72. After having revealed perfect enlightenment and led many kotis of beings to perfect rest, he himself will be extinguished like a lamp when the oil is exhausted. So is that vision.

73. Endless, Mangusri, are the advantages of the one who at the end of time shall expound this Sutra of superior enlightenment that I have perfectly explained.